GINA TRON

SUSPECT

WHISKEY TIT
NYC & VT

Published in the United States and Canada by Whisk(e)y Tit: www.whiskeytit.com. If you wish to use or reproduce all or part of this book for any means, please let the author and publisher know. You're pretty much required to, legally.

ISBN 978-1-952600-58-6
Cover design by Constance Lizati

A NOTE FROM THE AUTHOR

I've tried my best to represent the events and the emotional truths of characters in this book as honestly as possible. Names and characteristics have been changed to protect the privacy of others. I've tried to treat everyone in these pages respectfully and fairly. I am not aiming to avenge or shame anyone, particularly any actions of adolescents, myself included. Rather, the details of some of the included events are meant to paint a picture that I hope can give back in some meaningful way. I hope that those who see themselves within these pages feel less alone. More than that, I would love it if my experience could contribute to some of the larger conversations about bullying, mass shootings and copycat threats.

TABLE OF CONTENTS

PROLOGUE

The sound of frantic scribbling was making me queasy. With each pen stroke, my stomach gurgled like a vat of dangerous acid. Then the scribbling stopped. My friend ripped the paper out of her notebook. I took a deep breath. I read the message.

"You fucking fatass whore. I'm gonna fucking kill you. Love, the Trench Coat Mafia."

I shrugged and watched as my friend stood up, then made her way down the front steps of our high school, slithering through groups of our seated classmates. Shielding my eyes from the late afternoon sun, I tracked her shiny pleather pants on their journey. The sky was far too cloudless and the spring breeze too amicable for such a thunderous note. As I watched her place it on the windshield of one of the student vehicles, I was almost suffocating. I adjusted the spiked dog collar gripping my neck. The sun's rays had heated it up like a car seat in the glare. The rays were doing something else too: they were reflecting off the white piece of paper under the black windshield wiper. It glistened like an opal, waiting there for my former best friend to find it.

My best friend and my worst enemy, to reference the '80s homicidal cult classic *Heathers*.

*

It's almost impressive that someone can cram so much hate into such a short note: body shaming, slut shaming, a death threat *and* a reference to Columbine? Needless to say, it hasn't aged well! Was I an asshole for going along with it? Or maybe just a coward?

I was wearing a ring that said "psycho" at the time, and after that day and the furor it provoked, Psycho became my nickname among my high school peers. If, like me, you grew up in the nineties, maybe I remind you of the class Goth who you figured *could* shoot up the school, or maybe was even rumored to have threatened to blow it up.

Yeah, that's me.

If you're in school now, maybe I sound like one of your classmates who got arrested for terroristic threats. There are so many teens who have done crap like that; it's nothing special and I was one of them, but before you vilify or dismiss me, let me offer a little context. That note's language was normal vernacular for our crew of friend-enemies. Just one year earlier, the girl it was addressed to had written in my yearbook, "Trampina, Chinga [a boy I liked] is the biggest fucking faggot I've ever seen and I pray to God you get over him by next year." It was signed, "Your best friend."

It was the nineties after all, a time of rampant and normalized homophobia, a time when the effects of bullying were not taken very seriously.

The first time I watched the music video for Pearl Jam's 1992 hit "Jeremy," I was mesmerized. The video begins with closeups of black and white newspaper clippings, paired with snippets of audio that appear to be from news coverage. A flash of black and the word "harmless" is written on a chalkboard. A kid, presumably Jeremy, squirms in a wooden chair; he and the leering children surrounding him are all wearing white, like angels.   They point and laugh at him. He runs through the woods, in anguish. He stretches his arms out to a dark sky, orange flames raging behind him. Near the end of the video, Jeremy walks into the classroom, stands in front of the blackboard, and pulls something out of his pocket. The camera cuts to his classmates, frozen in place and covered in blood. I assumed this represented a school shooting, that Jeremy had slaughtered his classmates. What I didn't know was that because of MTV's restrictions on violent imagery, the channel had edited the original video to eliminate a scene of Jeremy placing the gun inside his own mouth.

When I learned this crucial detail, I felt a little disappointed to realize that the song was "just" about a suicide. "Clearly I remember/ Pickin' on the boy/ Seemed a harmless little fuck/ But we unleashed a lion," lead singer Eddie Vedder crooned. "Jeremy spoke in class today. Try to erase this/ from the blackboard." I'd assumed this meant he explained to them, through bullets, what they did to him. The fantasy of lashing out at those we perceive to have hurt us is attractive to those deemed harmless. It has the power to make the quiet one, the one who never spoke in class, finally stand out.

High school sucks. I bet you can relate to that. My high school experience as an outsider took me to the edge. I didn't actually want to kill anyone, but I eventually leaned into the reputation that I did. It didn't feel like I had another choice.

CHAPTER 1

FLATLANDERS

Let's go back to my first day of fifth grade, the day I met the girl who became my best friend — the one that vicious note targeted.

"Are you lost?"

I nodded. My body shaking, I stood in an empty carpeted hallway under hanging fluorescent lights. The lights were too bright and my heart was pounding.

"What classroom are you looking for?" the middle-aged woman continued. A teddy bear grinned from her peach-colored sweatshirt, sprinkled with tiny, fuzzy pills. I opened my mouth but nothing came out.

She tried again. "What is your teacher's name?"

"Mr. Carlman," I whispered.

"Okay, honey." She put a sympathetic hand on my back and guided me to a classroom without walls, its borders marked off with canvas dividers.

"Good luck, honey," she said, giving me a gentle push. She patted my head twice as I stood like a wide-eyed fawn in an open field. I felt my cheeks flush with embarrassment. Multiple pairs of blue and brown eyes glistened. My new classmates were sizing me up.

One girl giggled. Seated at a desk decorated in Lisa Frank gear, she had short frizzy blonde hair and bluebird eyes, crooked front teeth, and a galaxy of freckles across high cheekbones.

She leaned toward the girl sitting next to her.

"What a baby," she said.

This was Sarah, my future high school frenemy.

*

Having just moved to Vermont, I was the new girl in town. Yes, that mountainous, liberal state, void of billboards, home of sharp cheddar cheese and ice cream with chunks of pretzels and cookie dough in it. The reputed hippie haven and the land of Bernie Sanders.

In fact, the state is all that, but that's not *all* that it is. It's liberal for sure, but, just as happens in other places, the left-leaning people gravitate to cosmopolitan or politically comfortable zones. Often, the rural areas lean to the right. Today, they're Trump country.

In 1992, when I was 9, my family left Nassau County, Long Island—basically just an extension of the borough of Queens—for central Vermont. My parents bought a home in Barre, the state's "fourth biggest city" (calling it a city may be overly generous).   Even today, Barre's population is under 9,000. The town, where we moved,   also is home to about 9,000 residents. It may not be big, but as the self-proclaimed "Granite Center of the World," it is definitely proud. We moved to Graniteville, the part of the town with most of the granite quarries, where quarry explosions rocked our house during the day and coyotes' yipping put me to sleep at night.

White, deer-hunting Barre is more of a working-class town than the Birkenstock-wearing places most outsiders think of when they picture Vermont. In Barre, you can spot Confederate flags flapping in the wind, attached to the back of jacked-up pickup trucks. After the opioid crisis hit hard, the label *Scary Barre* gained currency; in fact, I took some credit for that nickname, as I'll explain later. Poverty nestled there, in colorful Victorian houses and dusty New England Capes downtown, and in trailers overlooking lush rolling hills and the small city center. This was a place that exalted high school sports stars above other objects in the civic firmament. From an outside perspective, all of this may sound quaint; at the end of the day, this *is* Vermont, after all, and the crime rate is impressively low. Many Vermonters, however, view Barre as a sinister crime haven. Drugs, break-ins and sadness: that's its rep.

Still, it functioned as a refuge from the violence that paralyzed New York City in the late '80s and early '90s, some of which also threatened Nassau County. My friend's brother was stabbed right by the high school I would have attended if we'd stayed, and there was a gang-related movie theater shooting not far from our house. My parents wanted a safer life for me and my brother and thought the rolling green hills of Vermont would provide it. Our new home in Barre was a split ranch that sat on ten acres off a dirt road, looking out over an assortment of hills, fields, and forests. We even had a view of Camel's Hump, one of Vermont's most beloved, highest mountains. Better than a view of your mob-connected neighbor beating someone up with a baseball bat on his front lawn.

Growing up in suburban Long Island, I'd always wanted to live on a farm. One of my favorite books was about a farm family. It featured illustrations of a woman milking cows and a redheaded boy feeding chickens. When I was seven, my dad took me to a feed store where baby chickens were for sale. The little chicks squeaked, running around on cedar chips. I touched their fuzzy bodies, warm from the red heat lamps, and begged my dad to buy me one. He had to drag me out of the store while I sobbed hysterically. I cried for hours and wouldn't let go of my dream of having a pet chicken, one that I could house-train and teach how to speak.

The veins on my right palm resembled the beak and head of a bird. I hoped this meant that having pet chickens was in my future. I figured I was right a year later, when my dad got a job offer and my parents sold our house. They bought the place in Barre and here we were.

It seemed like an easier life, but making friends was hard. My future friend Sarah looked at me from across the room with a scowl and a stare and rude comments, a stark contrast to what I was used to from classmates at my old school. When our teacher asked us to create a graphic response to a song that meant a lot to us, I picked Shannon's 1983 dance classic "Let the Music Play," a song I loved listening to while holed up in my pink Long Island bedroom blasting hot 97 on my purple boom box. Neon orange and hot pink boom boxes dotted my poster like colorful clouds, while Sarah had drawn guitars and an American flag to honor Bruce Springsteen's "Born in the USA."

I should have seen how different we were, but I couldn't. I think she must have, though: I overheard her call my drawing dumb and weird.

It wasn't school that brought us close, but God. Well, kind of. We both attended Barre's Universalist Church, the church with the highest steeple, full of thick brass pipes that looked like talons and a blood-red carpet. It was there that we first talked face-to-face.

It happened after a Sunday morning service while we were both snacking on the not-so-refreshing refreshments in the church basement. Everything was too dry or too bright, too stale or too moist. The sun seeped in through slit windows and blinded me. I squinted against the glare.

Sarah approached me. "My dad said you're a flatlander. And you pronounce words wrong because of it."

"Okay," I replied with an unconfident smile as I accidentally crumbled my dry blueberry muffin. Big crumbs fell to the ground, and I bent to pick them up. But more and more crumbs kept falling like flour-filled raindrops. Sarah laughed and walked off, leaving me standing there feeling like a lone dandelion that missed the lawnmower's blades.

At dinner, I asked my mom what a flatlander was.

"It's a term used in the hills or mountains to describe people from flat land. That is—well, that's what we are."

"So, is that a good thing or a bad thing?"

"It's not bad to be from somewhere flat, but I think here, it isn't a very nice thing to say."

"Oh," I said, puncturing a pea with my fork.

"Some Vermonters don't consider others to be real Vermonters unless their families have been here for multiple generations," my dad chimed in.

My brother, who was four, interrupted by grabbing a handful of Parmesan cheese and putting it in his hair, one of his favorite dinner pastimes.

"Goddammit, Matt, no!" My father scolded him.

"Dandruff," Matt giggled. Dad grabbed his arm and took him upstairs to wash his hair while I pondered what the generation thing even meant.

7thGnr8ionVTr would later become Sarah's AOL screen name.

My fifth grade teacher, I'd soon learn, wasn't fond of flatlanders either. That was funny, because he wasn't a seventh-generation Vermonter as Sarah proudly claimed to be. Instead, he was born and raised in a flat state. He once mocked me in front of my classmates as we were organizing a potluck party. I offered that my mom could make cannoli—or, as he put it, "flatlander food." Not only did he humiliate me and my peers, but he failed to do much teaching. It felt like he mostly talked about baseball and he never assigned homework, a stark contrast to what I was used to back in New York. In those days, I'd loved every minute of my homework.

Because I was an imaginative kid, I reacted by fantasizing that this teacher was an evil scientist with plans to kidnap and kill his students. I envisioned him kidnapping my crush and turning him into a robot. Teaming up with one of the cute boys from class, I would have to fight him off. He'd be arrested. Or killed. Because he was mean to me and an authority figure, I demonized him for my own entertainment.

*

I can't recall exactly when or how Sarah and I became friends. But at some point, she went from being a stranger who said mean things to me from across the classroom to a friend who said mean things to me in my bedroom. I remember the first time she tried to tell me how to present myself.

"All flatlander clothes," she said as she shuffled through my closet. One by one she clacked my red, yellow, and blue plastic hangers as she inspected each article of clothing. "Baby clothes," she said, pulling something off the rack: an extra-long colorful shirt displaying an ocean scene. Two neon plastic fish were sewn on with a large fluorescent string. A crab made of red puff paint grinned from the ocean bottom. In one of my drawers, I had a matching pair of fish scale biker shorts.

"I like it," I protested.

I was sitting on my bed wearing an off-the-shoulder white blouse with lace trim and a colorful barrette made of shoelaces. I loved my outfit. I didn't want to dress like

Sarah did, with her plain oversized cotton tee and matching loose shorts. I wanted to be colorful. I wasn't used to this. My friends on Long Island used to give me more freedom. On the other hand, they didn't pay me this much attention.

"I don't like many people, Gina. But I do like you! I'm just trying to help."

My cheeks flushed; I felt special when she said that. Maybe she liked me *more* than my friends back home.

"Remember, Gina, we'll be in sixth grade next year. People will be going to third base."

"I see," I said, looking around the room. I didn't know what that meant, but it was something sexual. When I'd asked her recently what a blowjob was, she made fun of me for days but never explained. I still thought it involved a hair dryer.

"God, your clothes are like doll clothes," she went on. "You gotta put some meat on those bones." She eyed the scrawny legs I was dangling off my brightly painted bed. "You know what would make you look less awkward? A haircut."

I grabbed the ends of my hair, which was dirty blonde with streams of vanilla pudding yellow. It was down to my butt, and knotted because I never brushed it. My wavy, tangled tresses were as wild as the neon colors I liked wearing. But Sarah seemingly wanted me to mute my brightness.

"A short haircut may make you look less skinny. Like, shoulder length."

Eventually, I cut my hair, and as summer ended and sixth grade began, my look seemed to dull. With the yellow strands cut off, I no longer had bright blond messy hair. I had muted mousy locks between blond and light brown. Having Sarah tell me what to do—the structure of that—was weirdly attractive. Even my mom didn't tell me

17

how to look. The choices had been endless. Now they were as clear as a Vermont sky on a cloudless night.

Sarah would often barrel into my bedroom as if it were her own, opening and closing drawers in my dresser and desk. She found my diary under a stack of papers in the top desk drawer.

"Dear diary," she read out loud, "school is going pretty good. I have a new best friend, Sarah."

"Sarah, stop!" I pleaded like a toddler, trying to grab the volume: pale pink with a black-and-white cat on the cover. Sitting on my bed, she pushed me down with one hand and continued her reading.

"Sarah, please stop!"

"Bla bla bla, the neighbors," she continued, skipping my kind words for the girls down the street, shitty people according to her.

I feared what I knew was next. The diary was an extension of myself, the only outlet for my true feelings.

"I really like a boy in my class. His name is Cory and he has the bluest eyes."

A cackling roar came out of Sarah's mouth like a lioness waterfall.

"You like that idiot? Come on, Gina. That would never work."

The next day in class, I felt like I was on a cliff, waiting to be pushed off by Sarah. I figured the minute lunch period came, all hell would break loose. Sarah was eyeing Cory. I could almost feel her planning what she would tell him. I looked at the clock. 11:57. With each jump of the second hand, I was closer to the edge.

And then, buzzzzz. It was twelve.

When the silence broke into chatter, Sarah burst like a balloon. "Gina wants to fuck Cory."

I closed my eyes and put my head down on my desk, but I could still feel the reaction from our classmates.

"What? What?"
"Yeah, I read her diary."

CHAPTER 2

RED MEAT IS GOOD FOR YOU

I was a flatlander. I didn't fit in. My accent was distinctively from New York with my pronunciation of words like "talk" and "water." And despite being white and moving to an area built up by Italian-immigrant granite workers, I was still too "ethnic"-looking for many of my peers in the 1990s. I had big features, big green eyes, and a prominent nose. Many Vermonters, and some of my classmates, assumed I was Jewish. Some called me a "Jew" in disparaging terms, and harassed me for having a "Jew nose." I got used to it the way I got used to so many other rude and terrible comments. I wasn't used to such a stark lack of diversity. My town on Long Island had been pretty white, for sure, but it wasn't totally whitewashed. There were people of color in my classes and on my block; I was friends with several of them.

And back on Long Island, my parents didn't stand out at all. In fact, they were as "Long Island" as you can get: Italian-American on one side and Irish on the other. Both were raised Catholic and lower middle class. Both were descendants of immigrants. Their friends were primarily either Italian or Jewish. Their friends, like my parents—my mother in particular—talked loudly, talked frankly, and would gesticulate with their hands. They also all pushed their kids, sometimes too much, to succeed. Here in

Vermont, my parents struggled to make friends and it's no shocker why. They came off pretty abrasively to the softer spoken Vermonters.

In Vermont, I was exposed to a lot of white Christians. And lots of snow. When I was ten, Sarah's dad took me on my first snowmobile ride. I hugged his cushioned midsection as we sped through the woods. Trees whirling past us, we glided over a powdery white blanket. My mom had said initially that she liked him because he reminded her of New Yorkers. And it was true that he never edited himself. He didn't sugarcoat anything. My uncle, however, came up for a visit and told me that he thought Sarah's dad was a hick.

"What's a hick?" I asked.

"You know, a redneck," he replied.

I didn't know what that meant, either, but I got the idea. My uncle said our neighbors were hicks too, which made more sense to me. They had a shipping container full of pigs that they slaughtered at the end of the summer; the boy was given a rifle at age nine. Soon afterwards, he pointed the weapon at one of his next-door neighbors. That certainly caused some drama on my dirt road.

Guns were everywhere in Barre, I was learning.

One day my brother and I were pumping high on our janky swingset when we saw one of the local ministers emerge from the woods that fringed the back of our house. Wearing an orange beanie, a rifle in hand, he walked towards us through the tall grass, an image straight out of *The Terminator.* My brother and I screamed and ran inside. That's how my parents learned they needed to post our property; it kept the hunters out.

There were plenty of guns at Sarah's place, too. My parents weren't down with that. In turn, Sarah's parents were not so fond of them, given that they were playing right into the flatlander narrative that native Vermonters loathed so much. They constantly talked about all the improvements they thought were in order—how central Vermont needed a GAP, more food options, and a better education system. This was exactly the kind of thing that native Vermonters didn't want to hear from someone new, especially someone from New York or New Jersey.

My mom also disapproved of Sarah's treatment of me, which of course only made me want to hang out with her more. Sarah was disrespectful, to boot. Other friends I had over the years would speak to my mother in a way that acknowledged her adult authority. I think it's fair to say that Sarah actually talked down to her.

Mom took us downhill skiing in Bolton Valley. On the drive over, the two of them fought about my diet.

"Red meat is good for you!" Sarah insisted.

"Gina hasn't gotten sick once since she's been a vegetarian!"

"She's probably sick right now! She's too skinny. She doesn't look good. She looks quite bad, in my opinion."

My mom straightened up, her mouth becoming a straight line. It was as if her lips sucked into themselves. I couldn't wait to get out of the car and ski down the slope in silence, away from them both.

When our ski adventure was done, Mom slipped on the ice while trying to get back into our car. It must have really hurt because it took her a while to get up. Sarah looked down at her and laughed. And what did I do? Nothing. I felt as frozen as the ice, and from Mom's perspective, I probably looked as cold. I could have lent her a hand, but I didn't, a choice I still regret. I may even have giggled nervously. I was too worried about incurring Sarah's wrath to do anything else.

Once we were on the road, I put the shameful event behind me as Sarah encouraged me to sing, to the tune of

"A Holly-Jolly Christmas," a song I'd made up called "I'm a Roly-Poly Puppy." My friend was often impatient with my hyper tendencies—and I admit I could be pretty annoying sometimes, as I still am to this day—but at other times she encouraged me and that felt rewarding. Right now she seemed to be in an extraordinary mood and I felt accepted by her. Mom was driving in a quiet rage and I guess I was okay with that. I resented her flatlander way of drawing negative attention to our family. She was making me, an awkward-looking, shy girl, into even more of an outsider.

Not long afterwards, Sarah's family came over to cross-country ski with mine on our property. During that outing, I watched Sarah's dad push her to the ground. She lay sobbing in the snow in her puffy jade jacket, a flannel hat over her blonde curls. I kept skiing, pretending I didn't notice. I was afraid she might lash out if I embarrassed her by helping. I felt weak, as weak as my skiing skills, and cold as the snow around us.

I didn't know how to help her but I did help take care of the six chirping chicks from a feed store nearby. For months before their arrival, I read books about raising chickens. Despite having educated myself about the intellectual capabilities (and shortcomings) of the birds, I was still naive. I turned a shoe box into a bed big enough for a baby hen. I intended to pick my favorite chick and keep her in my bedroom, and I still believed that if I tried hard enough, I could not only house train the bird, but teach her to speak English.

"There's no way in hell we are keeping a chicken in the house, Gina. You can't train a chicken to do anything. Their brains are the size of peas."

All six chicks were supposed to be female, but I knew that one of them would grow up to be a rooster. My parents rolled their eyes, but my premonition was correct.

Big Red matured into a vicious beast with a shiny red coat and floppy comb. He would rape the hens and use his talons to attack my brother and me.

Sarah's family said that us getting chickens didn't make us more Vermont-like. If anything, it made us less so. Just flatlanders playing farm.

Maybe they were right about that.

*

In addition to my mom disapproving of Sarah's influence on me, my parents were getting tired of her dad's prejudice. He became furious when the news came out that our church would openly and publicly welcome gay people. He hated that Mom wasn't similarly enraged.

"I think it's a good thing," I remember Mom saying into the phone. She was sitting on her queen-sized bed. Through the window I could see snow falling in slow white clumps. I had walked into the room to ask if I could take the snowmobile out. She didn't see or hear me yet. Her back towards me, she held the phone to her head full of dark curls. Then she hung up. "Bigot," I heard.

Mom always stood up for what she thought was right. She never let things slide to appease those she felt were in the wrong. She was a fighter and her family often dismissed her as an annoying "feminist," a woman hard to satisfy. She embarrassed me with her outspokenness. At the same time, I envied the ease with which she could be assertive, even aggressive. If I didn't look so much like her, apart from my hair, I might have guessed that she wasn't my biological mother. I thought at the time that if we had been peers, she would have bullied me. She told me stories of how she and her high school bestie were mean to certain people and regretted it later. I figured that she'd have dismissed me as a loser if we'd grown up together. I feared she thought that about me as it was.

In my own eyes, I was too weak to defend what was right, let alone stand up for myself. At one of Sarah's birthday parties, friends and I gathered around her dad to hear the tale of why he didn't like Black people. It was late August and we had spent the day in Sarah's pool. The other 12-year-olds and I were dripping wet, with turquoise and fuchsia towels wrapped around our awkward bodies. He spoke of a memory that "explained" his dislike. I don't know what prompted it.

"When I was at Spaulding High School, there was a Black kid in our class. He had a real attitude about him, that one. He was whiny, and he had that fucking victim complex."

I remember thinking that one man was not the ambassador for an entire race of people. That the guy Sarah's dad described was very likely the first Black person he ever talked to. But Sarah and everyone else seemed to accept the story as normal. A few girls nodded. I looked down at the grass and wanted to disappear. I wanted to tell Sarah's dad that what he was saying was racist, but I was scared of being yelled at and kicked out of my friend group. I thought they were all I had.

Vermont is the second whitest state in the union. Its liberal image doesn't exactly match reality. Liberalism is confined to pockets scattered around the state. A high school in Montpelier, for example, was the first school in the nation to fly the Black Lives Matter flag. But a scenic drive through the rural landscape just a few miles away will still reveal, along with Confederate flags and Trump signs, the faded black and white "Take Back Vermont" signs dating back to 2000. They began popping up all over the state after passage of a law establishing civil unions for same-sex couples. Our own neighbors had those signs on their lawns. The slogan was about so much more than just opposing recognition for same-sex relationships; it was native Vermonters' attempt to fight back against an influx of liberal, middle-class people coming from out of state. Flatlanders like my family, basically.

Vermont mirrors the nation when it comes to the fact that Black people are locked up at a rate drastically exceeding their representation in the overall population: nine percent of those in prison are Black, as are just one percent of all Vermonters[1]. This is just one striking indicator of the fact that Vermont often isn't receptive to people who are deemed different. I see a link between that attitude and Vermonters' lack of exposure to racial diversity. When visiting the state in recent years, I have gone for days or weeks without seeing non-white people.

Back in the 90s, it was worse. In our middle school class of 150, everyone was white-passing with the exception of one student. Sarah's dad said he was "okay" and that he didn't "act Black."

CHAPTER 3

CRUSHING

If movies taught me anything, it's that life owes you romantic fulfillment—provided you're nice enough, cool enough, or bold enough. As a pre-teen, I loved 1980s coming-of-age films. In *Fast Times at Ridgemont High,* the nerdy teen gets the pretty girl; just by being nice to her, he becomes a welcome contrast to the jerks she formerly dated. The two dweebs from *Weird Science* not only score babes, but steal them from their mean jock boyfriends. All it takes is a dose of confidence from a sexy woman they create on a computer. In John Hughes's *Sixteen Candles,* the unpopular protagonist played by Molly Ringwald is paradoxically depicted as having something special about her, even though at bottom she's totally unremarkable. Thanks to this specialness, she captures the class beefcake. In *Pretty in Pink,* Ringwald plays an unpopular, impoverished teen who falls in love with a popular rich boy. He worries about what others will say, but in the end, love prevails. I thought that these were reasonably accurate portrayals of teen life—which meant that someday (never mind the odds, given the pecking order at my school) my crush would love me back.

I met Evan, the target of my years-long obsession, in sixth grade. My class photo shows an 11-year-old me smirking because I'm too self-conscious to smile. Behind me is the familiar laser background, and on my small frame a black western-style shirt whose decorative fringe emphasizes the flatness of my chest. The decoration extends to little circular glued-on mirrors. This was a shirt that Sarah absolutely hated, one of my "flatlander" shirts from Long Island. I'm wearing the shirt in a group photo, too, standing in front of Evan along with my other homeroom classmates. His body language mirroring mine, he leans slightly to one side, arms down. My western shirt is set off by a white denim mini-skirt and black flats. Evan wears a flannel shirt that hangs on his frame. His eyes are wide. Our mouths share the same stoic expression, but my eyes are closed.

"Damn it, Gina," Evan said as he passed me in homeroom. "You messed up the picture!"

He smiled warmly, so I knew he was kidding. I giggled.

Other boys ignored me. The ones that didn't called me ugly or "retarded," or mocked me for being shy or "weird-looking." Because I was so quiet in class, it was easy to push me around. Evan, though, never said anything mean. He even made small talk, which amazed me. I loved to doodle, and he excelled at drawing. So naturally, I almost immediately started crushing on him. My heart would beat faster when he was nearby; when I sensed his gaze, I couldn't even think.

Our grade was divided into two teams, which meant that Sarah and I were separated, like the imitation silver halves of the BFF heart we wore on silver chains around our necks. She was upset; she wanted to be together. Somehow I became friends, albeit briefly, with an objectively more popular girl named Nadine. She had shoulder-length hair in a wavy perm and wore brightly-colored earrings. I loved her looping handwriting and her style. We bought matching earrings, large magenta squares with dangling turquoise squiggles inside. I wore them to class but would take them off before lunch, since Sarah and I ate together. The one time Sarah spotted me wearing them, she called them "ugly-ass 80s earrings." Not being in classes with her gave me a chance to wear what I wanted without getting hassled. But hassling ensued when Nadine spilled the beans that I had a crush on Evan. I tried desperately to pretend it wasn't true. And I continued faking that for months.

By March, Nadine asked if I still liked Evan. Lying, I shook my head no. That night I attended a dance at the local Elks Club, a brick building in downtown Barre. A crimson awning protected granite steps that lead to a hallway graced with a crimson carpet. In the ballroom, an elk's taxidermied head stared down at the dance floor. The stage was draped in majestic dark red curtains. The dance hall space was two stories high, the ceiling adorned with tiny square white panels. White streamers grabbed at the disco ball that dangled in the center of the room like a bridal silk spider.

As I entered, the bass was moving the room, strobe lights flashing insistently. When I spotted Evan in the swirl of bodies, my heart fluttered like a moth to a lamp. As the night wore on, my friends talked about which boys they wanted to slow dance. Sitting on a stool in the bathroom vanity of the venue's basement, I looked in the mirror while hesitating to express myself. I shrugged when asked who I wanted to dance with.

"Still Evan, huh? That black haired geek? You aren't good enough for him. Trust me, you'll see. You'll get knocked off your pedestal."

Soon enough, I was literally knocked off the stool. My friends brought me to sit at a table that offered a perfect vantage point on the stage of dancing couples. When I sat down I realized that I was staring straight at Evan dancing with Nadine. My friends, Sarah included, looked on as Nadine and Evan stared back at me. The look on Evan's face was hard to interpret: perplexed and intrigued, I decided. He never took his eyes off me as they slow-danced to Bryan Adams's song "Everything I Do." The six-and-a-half minute song felt like it lasted an hour. I just sat, unable to move, both entranced and nauseated. I kept trying to look away, but whenever I did, I could still sense Evan's eyes. I suddenly felt a bolt of paranoia in my gut that my friends had wanted me to see this, that they were relishing in this, because they enjoyed watching me suffer. That night I went home and cried, losing my emotional virginity to a completely new version of pain.

This moment had changed everything.

CHAPTER 4

BULLYING

I was painfully shy and I was embarrassingly sensitive. I was weak, passive, and followed the directions of others while wandering the hallways of my middle school, often feeling like a zombie looking for brains. A zombie who was too scared to even use the bathrooms to pee. I could barely speak in class. I never volunteered. When called on, I'd stutter and start to panic. Sometimes teachers would warn, referring to me, "You gotta be careful of those quiet ones!" I finally thought I knew what that meant when I heard "Jeremy," the Pearl Jam song I've previously mentioned. I later learned that it was based on Jeremy Wade Delle, a 15-year-old high school student who shot himself in front of his English class on January 8, 1991. Jeremy was described as "real quiet" and known for "acting sad." Eddie Vedder of Pearl Jam read about Jeremy's death and was inspired to write the song, which also drew on a memory of an old schoolmate of Vedder's who had shot up a classroom. It isn't clear whether the real Jeremy was bullied, but Pearl Jam certainly depicted him that way.

When I learned that the song was about self-inflicted violence and not a massacre of others, my thoughts spun off in a new direction. I figured that if I ever got sad enough to kill myself, maybe I should do it in school. In fact, such fantasies had been dribbling into my mind for the last couple years. I'd picture jumping from the roof of my middle school, the building where I experienced so much pain. If I killed myself in that spectacular way, maybe my tormentors wouldn't be able to erase the memory.

In 1996, fourteen-year-old Barry Loukaitis showed up at his high school in Moses Lake, Washington wearing a black trench coat and armed with two handguns and a rifle. He killed three; his algebra teacher and two of his classmates, then held an entire classroom hostage. Eventually, a gym coach subdued him. The prosecutors in Loukaitis's case pointed to the "Jeremy" video, particularly the edited version, as having influenced him. After the Columbine High School shooting in 1999, that video was wiped from network television.

Loukaitis wasn't the only one who claimed to be inspired by the video. In fact, it gained a bit of a cult following. There's still a website devoted to Jeremy Wade Delle's life and death, but mostly just his death. The site includes a map of the classroom where he died, showing where his blood pooled after he shot himself. Delle's father has stated that websites about his son often spread misinformation, and that they glorify the young man's decision to end his own life. When visiting Delle's grave, the father often finds that fans have deposited notes and artifacts.

Did Delle's death actually inspire any in-school suicides or homicides? That's hard to say. In 2019, a high school student in Oregon—a would-be real life "Jeremy," one could say—attempted to shoot himself in front of his classmates, but the shotgun he'd brought for the purpose malfunctioned. A coach disarmed and then embraced him.

Despite the lack of solid evidence that Pearl Jam's hit played any part in encouraging specific acts of violence, the uproar over the "Jeremy" video disturbed Eddie Vedder so much that he stopped making music videos for half a dozen years. The video's director, Mark Pellington, told an interviewer that the whole band was traumatized.[2] "I think Pearl Jam was very, very upset that this song about an alienated kid who killed himself was taken to be a glorification of guy who shoots his classmates."

It was unintentional that a network-mandated edit morphed a portrait of a suicide into a sketch of artful mass murder, but in one respect the message stayed the same. The lyrics said the other kids were at fault for bullying Jeremy until he snapped.

Even though I was bullied by Sarah, I continued to bond with her over our paradoxical situation of being both overlooked and bullied by others. We were nerds, and despite being very intelligent, we were unremarkable in all the ways that mattered to our peers. Things didn't improve when our parents tried to get us involved in sports.

"Sarah's dad is here, see you later," I yelled to my mom as I ran out the door wearing my red and white softball uniform. "Superstars," the back of the shirt read. Number 6. I squeezed into the narrow back seat of the oversized blue and white pickup truck. Sarah, next to me, was Number 12. Her legs were jammed against the back of the driver's seat, where her large father sat, wrapped in Carhartt.

"I want to ask Coach Lamarre if I can play shortstop again."

"He's not going to let you, Gina." Sarah assured me he would keep us in the outfield. "Because he sucks."

I said I hated the outfield. "It's *so* boring. And it's bullshit."

I looked at the rear view mirror to see if Sarah's dad would scold me. When he didn't object to my swearing, I continued.

"Coach Lamarre says only twelve-year-olds can play shortstop and pitcher. Well, that's crap! His daughter is ten and she's always pitching. I used to play shortstop back in Long Island. I think I was pretty okay."

Sarah agreed. In her view, our coach was just an ass who played favorites with the popular girls.

"I know! Why does he care? He's, like, 40! That's *so* weird!"

We drove through downtown Barre. Sarah's dad stopped the truck. A man was crossing Main Street at the crosswalk.

"Walk faster, you dumb n—" he mumbled. My eyes opened wide with shock. I knew he was racist but this was the first time I'd heard him, or anyone, use the n-word, outside of the movies. It felt jarring, like biting down hard on a popsicle. "I've been seeing a lot more of these around. You know what they say, with n— comes drugs."

I turned to Sarah, but she was unwrapping a Reese's peanut butter cup.

We spent that day in the outfield, as predicted. Bored as predicted, I looked up at the sky: bright blue with just a few puffy white clouds. I wished that one would turn into a rain cloud so I could just go home. When our team came up to bat, Sarah and I were last on the list. We sat on the bench chatting. Our teammates ignored us.

"Why does your dad use the n-word so much?" I asked. I would never, ever have said that word. My parents had told me it was one of the worst words on earth.

"Oh, that's just how he is. It's really annoying. He threw out my La Bouche CD the other day."

"What?"

"He said it was rap, and that rap is, ya know, n-word music."

"That makes no sense! It's not even rap! And even if it is, who cares?"

Sarah changed the subject, excitedly telling me about a really cool outfit she'd spotted in JC Penney.

"Oh ya?" I wiped my hands on my shirt. I'd tried to clean my cleats and they'd gotten covered with rust-colored dirt from the outfield.

"Jesus Christ, Gina. As usual, you're making a fucking mess," she scolded me before offering with enthusiasm, "Wide-leg sunflower pants. We should both get them."

She loved the thought of us matching. It made me smile.

"Of course, my pants will be like ten times bigger than yours. You're an extra small, and I'm like an extra, extra, extra large." I didn't respond. I felt bad that Sarah was so hard on herself about her weight, but I was clueless as to how I could comfort her. Did I even have the skills? My own mom didn't know how to comfort me when I was upset about, well, anything. My friend talked about her weight incessantly, and often told me she was jealous that I was thin. Sometimes I figured that was why she was mean to me, so I tried to cut her slack. Besides, one-on-one she could be okay. She was meanest when other girls were around. With an audience on hand, I became her prime target. Further confusing matters, she'd send conflicting messages: one minute she'd say I was pretty—prettier than her, at least. The next, I was weird-looking.

"I hope my mom lets me try those pills." Diet pills. She sounded wistful.

Then, the mood in the dugout shifted.

"You're a fucking whore!" It was our teammate Barb, a broad shouldered girl with sharp blue eyes and silver braces. She and another older girl were standing over

Christine, a round-faced, blue-eyed blonde a grade below us.

"I heard you fucked Kyle Matthews on the bus."

"That's just not true," Christine defended.

I tensed up.

"Ain't what I fucking heard. Heard he's not the first, either."

"Ya, you really whore around," Barb's friend chimed in.

Sarah laughed, cackled even. My heart started pounding. Suddenly the dugout was a cave with several dragons in it.

Crying, Christine ran over to her father in the stands. He listened to her, then stomped off to talk to our coach. They conferred for a minute, standing by the fence. Then the coach came over to the dugout. I thought he was going to yell at Barb and her friend, but he didn't even look at them. He walked right up to Sarah and me. His brow furrowed, his thick mustache quivering, he looked like he belonged in a Mario Brothers imposter game.

"Sarah and Gina, I need to talk to you *now*!" He took us behind the dugout.

"I heard what you two said. Christine is very upset."

I couldn't speak. "We didn't say anything!" Sarah told him.

"I heard you both called her some bad names."

"It wasn't us," I got out. "It was Barb and—"

He cut me off, said he didn't believe me. "You guys can either quit now or sit on the bench for the rest of the games."

Sarah looked at me. I tensed even more.

"Fine then," she said. "We quit."

Our teammates, including Christine's actual tormentors, cheered as we gathered our belongings and left.

"Those losers sucked anyway," I heard them say.

I was kind of relieved. I disliked my coach and pretty much everyone on the team, none of whom respected us. But I felt anxious about telling my parents that we'd been kicked out. How could I explain it? Sarah and I walked slowly back to the stands to tell her dad what had happened.

"I can't believe this," I told her, looking down at the thick crabgrass and dandelion leaves. "This is so messed up! I bet he knows it's not us." I kicked over a long, lanky weed sticking up from the shorter grass. "It's because we aren't very good. He just wanted an excuse to cut us."

"I know. And those bitches are."

"I can't believe we got kicked off the team for bullying that we weren't even doing! We get bullied by our teammates every day."

Sarah looked at the bright side. "I'm just glad we have each other. You're my best friend, Gina."

I felt like she'd flipped a light switch on in my heart. I smiled. "You are too."

"Wanna come over and hang for the rest of the day? I can show you those sunflower pants in my JC Penney catalog."

In the end, we both ordered pairs of sunflower pants. We bought matching hats, too: floppy hats, with a giant, fake sunflower glued on the front. We wore our twinsies outfits to school one day and got called lesbian lovers and losers. When we quit the basketball team we joined in middle school after it was clear we were unwanted, the team cheered. When we joined soccer, even our coach made lesbian cracks. I felt closest to Sarah when we were being bullied together. Even though she continued to bully me, we could bond over being bullied by worse bullies. Then it seemed like we were a fighting team, even though I failed to actually fight back. That wouldn't come until later.

Sarah and I also hung out with a small group of female friends. There was Donna, who with doe-brown eyes and braces, had a glow and a smile that could not be captured in any photograph. Then there was Betty, a vicious girl with mousy brown hair and crooked teeth. She was around five feet tall and lived in a trailer park. She picked fights with other girls and was mean to Donna and me on the playground. The funny thing was that she was a soft-spoken angel on the phone after school. We would talk like that for hours about life and clothes and boys, a stark contrast to how she treated me in front of our friends. Maybe she thought she had to uphold the pecking order. Even her own parents were bullies. When I visited her trailer, her sister called me ugly while her parents laughed at me. Later, Betty revealed to me that they were laughing because they also found me ugly.

Sarah and Donna and Betty, along with two others I'll call L. and M., made a memorable appearance at my twelfth birthday party. Memorable, but standard.

"Keep looking at them, ya dyke," M. invited. "Take a better look. This is something you clearly don't know anything about." I averted my eyes and shrank away. I hadn't meant to stare at her chest. I'd never seen naked breasts like that. They looked like they belonged to an adult. I didn't even change my own shirt, settling for paw print pajama bottoms. Sarah was in the corner, going through my desk drawers in search of my diary. I was uncomfortable, but trying to adapt, becoming somewhat numb to all this kind of behavior.

"It's opening presents time," my mom announced, her voice carrying through my thin bedroom door.

"It's opening presents time," Sarah mocked under her breath. If Mom could hear, she ignored it.

We sat in a circle on the living room rug. L. handed me a gift bag, green and iridescent. I took out a wad of coral tissue paper, shoved in there like a broken hydrangea. Inside were tiny metal ankh earrings, like in the Ace of Base music video for "The Sign."

"I love them," I said warmly, but L. and Betty looked disgusted. The Betty I talked to on the phone had disappeared. The other gift was a collective offering. I unwrapped a cold, mushy brown piece of plastic. It was fake dog poop.

"We were gonna get you a real gift," said Sarah, after Mom went upstairs, "but instead we shared nachos and drinks at Orange Julius with the money."

I squeezed the fake feces in my fist like a stress ball. I felt hurt and disrespected—but then thought I might be overreacting. Fake poop *is* pretty funny.

But: were they calling me shit?

Was I shit?

"Those are my old earrings," L. said. "I didn't even clean them."

I pointed out their gift bags in the corner. Mom had said I should give them party favors for coming, so we'd gotten them bracelets. They had different charms: a fake silver dolphin, a peace sign. My favorite was a sunflower.

They opened the gifts, briefly looked at them, and set them aside.

"Did you use actual tissues instead of paper?" Sarah asked.

"Yeah." I was confused.

"Gross."

I was getting a sinking feeling in my middle. I protested, "It's not like the tissues were *used*."

Sarah told me not to be such a fucking baby.

"Hey! You kids watch your language!" Mom shouted from the kitchen.

I had rented my favorite movies for the party: *Gremlins* and *Gremlins 2*. We only got to the part in the first one where the gremlins bulldoze through the drunk neighbor's home when Sarah shut it off.

"This is kid stuff," she said, and took off her T shirt. "Gina, you should take off your shirt, too."

I shook my head no.

"What's wrong?" Betty had her top off as well. "You don't want us to see how flat you are? Not like we don't know already!"

"At my last birthday party," Sarah said, "Gina changed into a dumb flamingo bathing suit and her body looked like a bean. No tits at all!"

I stared ahead at the black TV screen that just a few minutes ago was filled with loud green gremlins causing mischief.

"Come on," Sarah tugged at my sleep T. "Take off your shirt."

"What for?" I wasn't sure what would be worse: how my friends would react if I obeyed or if I didn't.

"Come on, Gina. Don't be a baby about   it."

Then, some of my friends held me down until they got the shirt off me, only to mock my body. Exposed, I slipped into my sleeping bag as Betty tried to roll the bag down while Sarah's laugh echoed off the small bedroom's walls.

After the girls left the next morning, my mom spoke to me.

"Gina, I can hear the way your friends talk to you. It's very upsetting. I don't like it. They don't respect you. I knew Sarah did that, but—"

"Mom," I cut her off, angry and embarrassed, "they respect me fine!"

40

I ran upstairs and spent Sunday sulking in my room, reading *The First Evil* by R.L. Stine, a book about cheerleaders being murdered.

On Monday at recess, my friends wouldn't shut up about how "stupid" my party was. Pacing in front of the swings, Betty mocked me, claiming I'd used toilet paper to wrap the party favors.

I said I'd used tissues, not toilet paper—and at least there were actual nice things in that wrapping, unlike what I'd received from them. "And it was *my* birthday, after all."

Betty approached the swing I was sitting on, looked me in the eyes, and punched me in the stomach. I gasped as she raised her fists like a boxer. Was she going to hit me again? When I cowered, she retreated. The others laughed.

"What was that for?" I was in pain and out of breath, one hand on my stomach, the other gripping the cold chain swing chain.

"For running your mouth and acting like a know-it-all bitch!"

"From now on we should call you Gremlin Girl," Sarah said, "since you're friggin obsessed with those childish movies. I told my dad about it and he asked, 'was this a seventh grader's party or a seven-year-old's?'"

Evan walked by, en route to the monkey bars. He locked eyes with me. I went mute. I didn't want him to hear or see me freaking out.

After recess came my favorite class: math. I sat behind Evan, and he often talked to me.

"I drew a picture of someone taking a crowbar to a car," he'd say.

Sometimes I couldn't understand him because he mumbled, and I was too shy to ask him to repeat anything. It still made me giddy.

"Look at these new pens my dad got me," he whispered, as the teacher talked about fractions. Pivoting around, he rested a piece of lined paper on my desk and drew an illustration of a man with a chainsaw. Blood drawn in red ink dripped from the saw's spiky blade. I smiled. Evan's violent drawings and his mumblings were my saving grace. That and the class known as PSTL (pronounced "pistol," for Problem Solving Through Literature) and, sometimes, the writing I did in my diary, even though I'd often rip it up to prevent Sarah from finding out my secrets. Though, she was well aware of my crush on Evan; it was hard to conceal. At one point I made a "to kill" list. On it were the names of my meanest middle school friends. While I didn't actually want them to die, I wanted them to stop hurting me. After a few weeks of it existing, I ripped that up, too.

My anxiety over the bullying was stoking compulsive thoughts and behavior. The day that Betty punched me, I sat at my bedroom desk and wrote a line for each syllable in the question I'd asked her, "What was that for?" I would often go over my recent interactions, trying to pinpoint what I'd done wrong. How could I better improve my social standing?

I closed my eyes and thought of Evan. That helped me relax. He and my mother were my mainstays, even though I couldn't really talk to him, and Mom was often too stressed to fully listen. I thought that they were the only ones who at least had good intentions. They were two lamps I looked to, hoping they'd guide me down the dark, confusing hallways of my life.

When I was in eighth grade, Mom sat me down on our pink living room couch, which nobody ever sat on; typically, we all sat on the food-stained white and blue couch in the den, perched in front of the television. She said she had something important to tell me.

"That lump I found, it turned out to be cancer." Her green eyes, so similar to mine, were welling up.

Warmth trickled up my body, and my breathing changed. I didn't know what to say.

"I'm gonna be sick for a while, but it will be okay."

She put her hand over mind. I tensed at the touch.

"I'm going to do some chemo, and I'm going to lose my hair, but it will grow back."

I shut down, as though that could prevent this from happening.

When I told Sarah on the phone, she also went quiet. Then she began talking about an outfit at JCPenney. She didn't like my mom, so I didn't expect much sympathy. In that moment, I resented both her and Mom for resenting each other.

Around this time, I had to write a series of vignettes for my PSTL class. The assignment was connected to our reading of Sandra Cisneros's *The House on Mango Street.* I typed them up, taped the printouts onto a cube (an old UPS box that I covered in paper), and added black and white photos, mostly taken by me. The exception was one of my mother taken by my dad in the 70s, shortly before they were married. In this picture she is 20, sitting at a vanity, wearing a frilly white shirt with embroidered floral details. Her mouth is slightly open, a model's pose. Her straight black hair is parted in the middle. She'd told me she used to spend hours ironing it to flatten the natural curls.

When it was my turn to give the dreaded presentation about my vignettes, I spoke about my brother, how he loved video games. I talked about my dad's gardening. Then I got to mom and felt sad. What if she was going to die? My classmates, unaware of my distress, perked up at seeing her photograph.

"Oh, wow, Gina's mom is gorgeous!"

"She looks cool, too!"

As I walked back to my seat, I heard one girl say to another, "How the hell did that woman give birth to *that*?" The other girl laughed and made a show of ogling me.

My peers, who barely talked to me, seemed so eager to hang out with my mother of the past. My mom was so much cooler than I am, I thought. Why couldn't I have inherited that? Then I felt guilty for being jealous of a woman who was gearing up for chemotherapy. Despite her illness, my own well-being and education were still at the forefront of her mind. I didn't say I was being bullied, I even denied it when she asked, but she must have noticed my mood swings and my lack of confidence. And of course she'd seen the way my friends treated me whenever they came to our house.

I hated being bullied, yet accepted it as normal. It had become part of my reality. Much later, I would seek explanations for these experiences. I'd spend hours in my college's library looking through sociology books for information on females who bullied their own gender, their own friends. I found very little. It was as if the phenomenon didn't exist. Apparently male bullying, because it was more obvious, aggressive, and physically violent, got all the attention, while female bullying was easier to ignore. Less in the way of black eyes, more bruised hearts and hidden pain. I was delighted with the 2002 publication of *Queen Bees and Wannabes* because it thrust the topic into the spotlight. It also partly inspired the film *Mean Girls*.

Recent studies have shown that girls and women tend to use relatively indirect methods when bullying each other.[3] These include rumor-mongering and exclusionary behavior. While young males, just like adult males, may kill with weapons, young female bullies more often resort to verbal and social battery. Regardless of gender, however, the intent is often the same.

"Motivation for both groups usually includes: a desire for power, for control, for achieving greater social status and popularity," according to a *Psychology Today* report.[4] Although some use violence for an assist in climbing the social ladder, it is rarely resorted to by the bullied as straight up revenge for abuse they've endured. Therefore, it's unlikely that the procession of young male shooters I watched on TV in the late 1990s were real-life versions of the Carrie of movie fame—a high school student who bloodily avenges unbearable harassment by her classmates.

Still, I came to feel as much compassion for those boys—heads down, doing their perp walks—as if they were that fictional character, wronged over and over until they were pushed past the edge of sanity.

CHAPTER 5

MAYHEM

It took a bomb blast to trigger my fixation on darker things. The fertilizer and shrapnel were already there inside me, but carnage in Oklahoma City set them off.

My family and I were visiting Long Island relatives on April 19, 1995. I was standing in my aunt's mustard-yellow kitchen, which stank of garlic and sour dish rags, when I saw the first televised images of the destruction visited on the Alfred P. Murrah Federal Building. Even though the TV set was small, the larger-than-life effects of the explosion sucked me in. One entire wall of the building seemed to have collapsed, revealing broken glass and filing cabinets and dangling electrical cords—and, most importantly, trapped people on upper floors peering down at the horror below. Helicopter footage showed ranks of cars in flames. They were dented, as if a monster truck had rolled over them. Thick black smoke billowed up from the site.

From then on, I was glued to the television. I sat on my aunt's multi-color shag rug watching CNN as children were carried out of the rubble. One kid's head was wrapped in fabric like a mummy, streams of blood all over the little face. Shoes rested on piles of debris. My brother lay beside me on the floor playing Game Boy. I couldn't look away from the screen. It felt like everyone in the world must be watching, my classmates Evan and Sarah and Nadine included. It made me feel connected to others I knew and to the world at large.

This was the pivotal moment that confirmed my growing passion for true crime stories and media coverage of atrocities. (I'd felt a tinge of it before, when Selena's "I Could Fall in Love" came on the radio and Sarah informed me that Selena had been murdered by a friend, information that strengthened my love for her music.) That night I lay on my aunt's pull-out mattress. The sharp bedsprings creaked every time I moved. I couldn't sleep. I felt the urge to go downstairs and turn on the news. There hadn't been any dire developments in the last few hours before my mother peeled me away from the warmth of the television set, but I wanted to watch for updates anyway. It was the first time I really paid attention to the news. I needed to know more and I needed to know why. How could somebody hurt so many people? I'd seen images of war, but the fighting took place in other countries; the issues were things like struggles over land, or freeing people from concentration camps. Who would do this to a city in Oklahoma?

The death toll was high, but I'd thought it would be much higher given how decimated the building looked. 168 people died, and over 680 others were hurt. Timothy McVeigh, who had parked a yellow Ryder truck with a five-ton fertilizer bomb in front of the building just as parents were delivering their kids to an on-site daycare center, was arrested 90 minutes after the explosion on unrelated charges: driving a car without a license plate and lacking proof of insurance. McVeigh sported an interesting T-shirt. On the front was a sketch of Abraham Lincoln and the words uttered by John Wilkes Booth during the assassination: *Sic semper tyrannis* (Thus always to tyrants). On the back was a Thomas Jefferson quote: "The tree of liberty must be refreshed from time to time with the blood of patriots and tyrants."

As the Columbine High School killers would do a few years later, McVeigh used violence to make a mark. He knew that the key to having a real impact was to kill indiscriminately, telling his co-conspirators that there needed to be a body count if the goal was to make people pay attention. The bombing he pulled off is still considered to be the deadliest act of domestic terrorism in the United States.

Despite the patriotic claims of many domestic terrorists, in the end they turn their weapons on their own people. In that sense, their crimes could be interpreted as self-harm. Much the same thing is true of the school shooters of America. The target is only ostensibly "the other." In reality, it becomes the collective *us*.

"Did you see the news? It's so fucked up." I asked Sarah as I poked a veiny chicken nugget on my lunch tray. There was something red in its middle that looked like an artery.

"I know. We have to do something to help."

Sometimes, Sarah would reveal great qualities like this. She loved to get involved in social causes, and she adored animals. She'd encouraged me to volunteer with her at the local animal hospital over the summer.

On Sarah's initiative, the two of us, from our humble position as seventh graders, conducted a book drive on behalf of a public library located near the Oklahoma City blast site. The library had suffered damage and outright destruction of a large percentage of its volumes. Our project was wildly successful. Parents, students, and random community members donated children's books, hardcover classics, and sensationally-written paperbacks. The school newspaper wrote a story about it: "From Our

Children to Their Children." An accompanying photograph shows Sarah and me typing on thick-screened computers in the school computer lab.

The book drive was part of a project the two of us did for PSTL on our own time. As I've mentioned, this was a reading and writing class. It was aimed at so-called gifted kids. In PSTL we got to do creative writing alongside our reading assignments and book reports. I felt challenged in this class; my mother encouraged me, and the co-teachers really seemed to support me. I looked up to both of them, but especially Ms. Scharf. She wore glasses and beads, and was a lover of the arts. She seemed so different from most of my other teachers.

At the end of the year, Ms. Scharf wrote in my yearbook, "To the artist of the group—You're going to go far with your talents."

Evan also signed the yearbook. In the middle of a page filled with pen signatures from nerdy girls, "have a great summer" looked back at me in pencil. Evan had dotted the "i" in his last name with what appeared to be an upside down heart with a lightning bolt through it, a storm cloud overhead. He'd stopped me in the halls, exclaiming, "Gina, you just have to sign my book!"

Sarah wrote that I had changed her life and pleaded with me to "never, ever CHANGE." The word "CHANGE" was emphasized by several rounds of pen loops. At the same time, she crossed my face out in my yearbook picture, prompting my mom to become distraught.

"It represents hostility towards you," Mom theorized.

"It doesn't represent anything," I assured her. "It's a joke, Mom. Take a joke."

In my scrapbook from that same time, I proudly taped in a letter dated July 10, 1995: "On behalf of the Metropolitan Library System and the children of

Oklahoma City, thank you for the three wonderful boxes of books you and Sarah collected... This expression of love and compassion means a great deal to our library and to our community."

I enjoyed how the book drive connected me more closely to the recent tragedy. I, too, was now part of that gash on America's psyche.

Even though I didn't comprehend the politics behind atrocities like the Oklahoma City bombing, I couldn't look away from the TV coverage, and I couldn't stop seeing the images in my mind even when I lay in bed in the dark. I liked absorbing events that seemed big and confusing. My life felt so boring; I lived vicariously through the tragedies of others. I related to the victims and was intensely curious about what drove the perpetrators. There were plenty of both to go around. In the 1990s, it seemed like America was untouchable from the outside. No other countries' bombs reached our land. The only ones threatening Americans were other Americans, and it boggled my mind. I found domestic terrorism fascinating partly because it felt like a person attacking their own family members. And I was also intrigued by those more intimate attacks, when people killed each other at home or in their offices and schools. I wanted to know why anyone would commit such crimes.

But—"Jeremy" aside—I didn't think of kids as killers until a spate of school shootings crossed my radar.

In 1997 and 1998, there were four multiple-fatality school shootings: Pearl, Missouri; West Paducah, Kentucky; Jonesboro, Arkansas; and Springfield, Oregon. In West Paducah on December 1, 1997, Michael Carneal, then only 14, opened fire on a group of students in a prayer circle. Three died and five were injured. Before taking action, he wrote in a school assignment that his peers "mocked and slaughtered my self-esteem."[5] The event provided an early catalyst for the narrative that bullying creates school shooters; it was said that perhaps the carnage could have been prevented if only his teachers had heeded his "disturbing writing." Michael had reportedly composed a short fictional story in which he imagined himself killing the "preps" of his school.

On March 24, 1998, Mitchell Johnson, 13, and Andrew Golden, 11, pulled a fire alarm in their Arkansas school and opened fire as people tried to exit the building. A teacher and four students were killed. Ten others were injured. At the time, it was America's deadliest school shooting. Tried as juveniles, the boys ended up serving less than a decade behind bars. In response to what were viewed as outrageously brief sentences, Arkansas law was soon changed to ensure that future youthful attackers would face harsher punishment.

Even though the boys' motives remained obscure, I filled in the blanks and assumed they were getting revenge on school bullies. Something bad must have happened to make these kids snap, I thought. They looked to me like a 1990s version of my movie favorite Carrie, the brainchild of   Stephen King.

As a pre-teen, I repeatedly watched the movie that bore her name. My mother was very excited to share this lurid fairytale, and while I questioned her judgment, I fell instantly in love with the story's premise. Holy shit, the assholes in this school are like the assholes in *my* school, was my first reaction. Nothing could be more iconic than that mousy-haired outcast covered in thick blood, clenching her fists in agony on the stage of her prom. The preceding action perfectly illustrated how she ended up feeling the need to kill for revenge. Carrie was mistreated by classmates, teachers, and even her own mother. Then a group of students had the nerve to humiliate her further by rigging the prom queen election to ensure she would win, only to have a bucket of pig blood dumped on her head.

Watching that film was the first time I felt sympathy for anyone who'd commit such a drastic act. Before *Carrie*, I'd imagined murderers as serial killers, stalkers who crept in the shadows, disguising their voices when making threatening phone calls. They were adult white men with dark features and tattoos, like the bad guy in *Cape Fear*. They were predators; they were distinctly Other. Now I was noticing that kids my own age, freshly made humans sitting on plastic school chairs, could be Murderers as well. And if Mitchell and Andrew wanted revenge, I could definitely relate. Sometimes I fantasized about getting revenge on my bullies: not by killing them, but by either punching them or becoming a famous model to humiliate them—or, yes, jumping off the school roof. Anything to show them what they did to me and how wrong they were to do it.

And who did I want to prove wrong the most? My own mean friends.

But I'm getting ahead of myself. It took me time to transform from a civic-minded seventh grader into the angry girl who would be labeled a potential terrorist. That process involved my fraught transition to high school.

Mom, who had long since transferred my little brother to a Catholic school where he stopped being bullied the way he was in public school, wanted me to enroll in a private high school nearby. But I thought private school was for snobs. More importantly, I couldn't stand to leave Sarah. On my own, it seemed to me, I'd be too weak. I needed her—and I had to be near Evan. I couldn't imagine doing without that. Just the comfort of knowing that Evan and I would be in the same building was a driving force for me.

So I vetoed Mom's idea and chose Spaulding High School, a large public school with a shit reputation across the street from a tire store where teens gathered to smoke cigarettes. Despite my sporadic revenge fantasies, I was still too fearful to take any risks. What tactics could convince my friends and the world that the mistreatment I suffered was not only wrong but unendurable? Would it take violence? Would it take me being successful? What would it take to make me really matter? I had no idea.

CHAPTER 6

FREAKS

When I think of my transition to full-fledged teenager status, I often think of *My So-Called Life*. One of my favorite shows in middle school, it's about a 15-year-old girl named Angela Chase who dyes her hair a Manic Panic red. Exerting power through self-expression, she ditches her past along with her mousy look. Though cooler than formerly, she's still considered a "weird" girl and her new appearance muddles up her relationship with her childhood friend, parents and neighbor. Looking back, it seems absurd that a slight change in appearance caused such a ruckus in one's young life but it was the nineties and I for one can vouch that it's a realistic storyline.

I could relate to Angela Chase. But I also thought a lot about a more sinister character: my old friend Jeremy from the Pearl Jam video. I had anger inside of me, a drive to express it. At the same time, I wanted to spread my wings and socialize. I aspired to stand out while simultaneously fitting in. So far, I felt like I was failing at both.

Long before I was individually feared, my incoming high school class was regarded with apprehension by many adults in Barre. We were the class of 2000: a class of more than 300 kids, very large for the area, representing a combination of kids from Barre City with others from more rural schools like mine. Barre City was supposed to be rough; I'd heard rumors that a lot of those kids lost their virginity at 12. But the fact was that my own Barre Town class wasn't exactly known for docility. Just the year before, we'd gotten into big trouble for a giant snowball fight during which a few of my classmates stuck razor blades into the icy projectiles. Or so went a rumor I heard, unconfirmed. Our collective reputation was cemented: hard and cold as our fabled weaponry.

Not mine, though. I was more like sleet—somewhere in the middle, not hard enough or smooth enough. I'd sit in my room the summer before high school, giving off whiffs of summer sweat and Secret Powder Fresh deodorant, sniffing the inserts of Calvin Klein Eternity in my glossy issues of *YM* and *Teen Magazine*. I yearned to wear the clothes I saw in the MTV ads. Nada Surf's video "Popular," supposed to be a satire on the shittiness of high school, got me dreaming of becoming a cheerleader despite my past sports failures. Besides, Sarah had asked me to try out with her, so did I really have a choice?

In the fall of freshman year, we tried out for the varsity team. Neither of us made it, which didn't surprise us. But we still cheered enthusiastically for the sports heroes of Spaulding. In a photograph taken that year on "Spirit Day" of Homecoming Week, I wear a crimson school jacket with blue stripes on the sleeves, my name embroidered in white. My sun-splashed face is greasy from face paint: on one cheek a red peace sign and on the other *Go Tide* in blue (since Crimson Tide was Spaulding's athletic nickname).

I dyed my boring hair a dark auburn shade. I would have chosen a more extreme color, but I didn't think Sarah or other classmates would go for that. I wore mascara and LipSmack lip gloss and sometimes a bit of white eye shadow. For a game or dance, I'd decorate my eyelids with glitter. My outfits, though still subdued, took on glimmers of style. I loved wearing a metallic silver skirt from Delia*s, a catalog-only boutique I adored. One time I was wearing a shimmery turtleneck and a senior girl, passing me in the hall, complimented me on it. That made me feel like I'd been dipped in silver. Most of the time, though, I felt harassed on the bad days and ignored and dismissed on the good ones. At dances, I'd watch my peers from the sidelines as they paired up and swayed in each other's arms.

My mom assumed I was doing better at fitting in, and deduced that I must be picking up bad habits.

"Mom, I'm *not* smoking," I said.

She sat at the kitchen table, a pile of mail in front of her, wearing a blue turban around her bald head. She only had one more round of chemo to go.

"You smell like cigarettes sometimes." She'd become obsessed with this issue.

"It's the school bathrooms," I said, still holding my backpack, one foot on the stairs. I wasn't lying. I hated using the bathrooms, but sometimes I couldn't avoid it. I'd walk into a thick cloud of smoke and pee as fast as I could while overhearing girls boast about the boys they were having sex with.

"Come on, you're fourteen." She batted her eyelashless eyes. "I know you've smoked by now, you can tell me."

I was embarrassed that I'd never even tried a cigarette. I'd never been offered one. Part of me wanted Mom to believe that I smoked so she'd see me as cool enough to be a "normal" teen.

"Can I go up to my room now, please?" I tapped my toe, one hand on the banister.

"I got a package from Camp Exploration today. Take a look," and she held out some brochures.

"I told you, I don't want to go to that nerd camp." But I reluctantly took them.

"You really should repaint those nails."

I looked down at my chipped sparkly purple nail polish."

"I like them like this." I glanced at the stock photos of blond kids smiling next to a list of offerings: nightclub night, cruise ship night, whale watch, Museum of Fine Arts tour. Since I had no confidence that I could make friends, I figured that if I went there, I'd be all by myself. Which would make the most exciting events seem pretty pointless.

"You're going to that stupid nerd camp?!" Sarah exclaimed, her knees practically touching mine under our conjoined desks, which were covered with graffiti and blobs of chewed gum."I don't have a choice." I shrugged. "Mom signed me up. She thinks I smoke. She won't believe me when I tell her it's the smell from those damn bathrooms."

"All those grubs sparking up. Well, whatever. Your mom doesn't have the best judgment," Sarah concluded. The "grubs" were the underclass of our school. They were mostly from poorer backgrounds, many in foster care. They smoked cigarettes out in front in the mornings, creating a mushroom cloud of mingled smoke and cold breath. Often they simply skipped school. It just wasn't a priority for them, and no wonder. The average teacher, I noticed, barely acknowledged their existence.

I had to agree with Sarah that my mom could be a real pain in the ass. For instance, she'd been unhappy about the ersatz edition of *Great Expectations* assigned in my English class. The text had been shortened, the language simplified; she called it a "dumbed-down version." She complained vigorously to the school administration. The local newspaper ended up running an article about it; I keep a copy with the other, later articles that mention my family. In the end, I got to read Dickens's original text, though as far as I remember the rest of the class continued with the version that Mom objected to. My teacher seemed to hold her actions against me. Looking back, I think it was brave to make a fuss, but at the time I heartily wished she hadn't intervened.

Now Sarah scoffed at my lack of resistance. "You'd just be with a bunch of brats at that camp. I bet most of them are gonna be Massholes."

Mom said I had to go, and a part of me wanted to, but I was scared at the thought of having to manage without Sarah. Being away from my family, on the other hand, might have its good points. My mother's cancer recovery was stressing me out. She wanted me to take on more of a caregiving role and I didn't know how. I yearned to be free, free from feeling like I was failing at helping Mom through cancer, and—if the truth be known—free from my best friend, whose astrological sign just happened to be Cancer. At that age, I paid attention to sun signs. I was a Libra who felt weighed down, as if slabs of Barre granite had been piled high on my emotional scales.

Mom wanted me to act like an adult and Sarah wanted me to dress like a frumpy old woman. I wanted to act and dress like the teenager I was, in short skirts, tube tops, and other skimpy outfits—the way Kelly dressed on "Married with Children." And I didn't just want to look sexy and fun, I wanted my clothes to communicate my interest in the darker side of life. I loved "Real World," an MTV reality show about a group living situation, and on "Real World: Boston," which aired in 1997, someone named Elka was one of the roommates. I didn't connect with that boring brunette, but I loved the echo of Elks

Club in her name. I began to fantasize about an alter ego: Elka, who was outspoken and badass, the opposite of Gina.

In my desire to be cooler, I was drawn to a girl, Tonya, I'd admired from a distance when we were in eighth grade. Back then, my admiration of her style had been obvious enough for Sarah to accuse me of being a "dyke" over her. Towards the end of my freshman year at Spaulding, she and I were assigned to the same small group in our French class. She was wearing black leather pumps at the time, with black pleather pants and a neon green sweater. She looked exactly like I thought a popular girl should, like the pictures in *YM* and *Seventeen*. But at our school, the popular people wore boring clothes: straight leg jeans and North Face vests.

Sitting this close to Tonya made me nervous. I wanted to be her friend.

"I like your patch," I blurted, indicating the Marilyn Manson patch sewn onto her iridescent black backpack. I hadn't met anyone else who liked his music.

We chatted about which albums we preferred. I told her I was loving "AntiChrist Superstar."

"You two listen to Marilyn Manson?" One of our classmates was scandalized.

I shrugged. Tonya hesitantly nodded.

"That's for freaks," the girl said.

Freaks. It felt like a step up the social ladder—a major one, in fact. I thought of the Manic Panic ads I'd taped up on my bedroom wall: teens with brightly colored hair going wild at rock shows. At least freaks were badass.

"You're going to do fine." Mom kissed the top of my head. I was sitting on a bed in my dorm room, unpacking the posters I'd brought along to camp.

When she and Dad left, I fought the urge to chase them down the hall and beg them to take me home. I looked over at the other bed with its thin blue mattress, worrying that my roommate would shun me.

Hoping I could feel at least a little at home in the coming weeks, I taped up a poster for the band Bush, along with the CD jacket from a Marilyn Manson album. I made up my bed with black sheets, all wrinkled and puffed at the corners. After hanging up my clothes, I sat next to the open window, breathing in the sticky July air. From up on the third floor I had an excellent view of the Wellesley campus green. Dozens of campers had started to gather, laughing and chatting, some sitting on the grass. Weezer played from a portable radio. My chest squeezed tight at the idea of going out there. It looked so easy, I thought, for all those other kids, who were probably friends already, before they came to camp. And Sarah had told me I wasn't a likable person. That she wasn't, either, but at least we had each other.

Eventually, my roommate arrived: a smiling sporty blonde with a rolling suitcase. Her blue eyes sparkled; her cheekbones were high. What a snob, I concluded.

"Hi! I'm Penny."

I stood to accept the firm handshake, introduced myself, then waited for her to insult or ignore me.

She scanned my wall decorations, asked where I was from.

"Vermont."

"Oh, cool. I have never met anyone from Vermont before."

I smiled shyly. "It's only like two hours from here— the part where I live, anyway."

Penny turned out to be from Boca Raton, Florida. Two of her friends from there were also registered at camp, but "we didn't want to kill each other, so we're rooming separately," she said with a laugh.

Soon she suggested we go down to the green. She was being so nice, I thought it might be a setup.

On the stairs, I asked about her other friends.

"Nicole, you'll like her," she said. "She also likes Marilyn Manson. I don't know why, no offense, but I don't get that band. Too dark for me, but whatever. And Tara, I've known her since we both were five."

"Oh cool," I said.

"Delia*s?"

"Huh?"

"Your shirt."

I looked down at my mesh tank top. The top half was iridescent green and featured a tiny rainbow.

"Yes." I was surprised. Nobody at Spaulding even knew what Delia*s was.

"I like your shoes, too."

Sarah hated my chunky black platform sandals; it seemed like everyone did. Whenever I wore them, I heard multiple comments about "orthopedic shoes."

As we walked onto the green, I noticed one girl with pink streaks in her blond hair. She was wearing a dog collar, thin and black with tiny silver spikes. I tried not to stare, but I was definitely intrigued. Some kids were dressed like a more extreme version of Tonya. A group of them were wearing all black. I fell in love with the look of a Nine Inch Nails shirt paired with a long black velvet skirt. It matched how I felt.

In the nineties, as grunge faded into the background, what was considered "cool" by the mainstream became very plain: slightly flared denim and solid spaghetti strap tees. Wide leg JNCO jeans were the mark of those who dabbled in alternative subcultures. Everything that attracted me, those JNCO jeans included (an unfortunate choice, since baggy pants on someone as short as I am are a guarantee of unsightly, filthy pant leg bottoms), was looked down on as weird. And to add to my misfortune in being attracted to clothes considered offbeat in most parts of the country, I lived in Barre, Vermont. Maybe in a more thickly populated place, I could have located fellow freaks, even a crowd of them to hang with. A freak crew with whom to explore gradients of freakdom.

At camp, though, I felt like I was dreaming. I made friends, and did it all by myself. They actually seemed to like me for who I was. And whether or not they were deemed losers at their respective schools, they all seemed ultra cool to me.

One afternoon, we sat in a square on the green—Penny, Nicole, Tara, and I. Nicole placed her Discman in the center. She plugged in portable speakers, which I'd never seen before, and popped in a CD by L7, a group that influenced many riot grrrl bands.

"I'm thinking of getting black streaks," I told them, tugging at my hair. It currently sported some faint purple streaks I'd added in a weak attempt to be bold.

"That would look cool," Nicole said. She was wearing black velvet pants and a fitted black with an image of Marilyn Manson, his red lipstick smeared. A choker—deep purple velvet with tiny spikes—clasped her neck.

Penny agreed. "Not my cup of tea, but I think the style would look very good on you." She had on a polo shirt, diamond studs in her ears.

"Thanks." I smiled, still not used to their reactions. Instead of treating my fashion ideas as little short of criminal, they took me seriously.

Nicole said she might shave the back of her head. "Just the part underneath." She lifted her cherry red hair and pointed to the spot.

"So it'll be like a kiwi again." Penny turned to me. "Last time she shaved it, I could *not* stop rubbing her head. A little rub for good luck!"

"It worked for your final exam."

"Yes, it did. You'd better do it right before our SATs."

They were smart, rich, *and* they liked "freak" clothing. That combination was unheard of at Spaulding, where people assumed that dressing outside the norm was evidence of a bad home life.

We were joined by another girl from our dorm floor. Reshma was a genius at applying eye liner. It was black and so thick; she had perfect wings, little black upturns at the outer corners of her wide hazel eyes.

"Hey ladies," she said. "You all gonna do something for the talent show on Friday?"

We weighed various possibilities. Then Tara proposed, "We could do something funny. Like, as a group or something."

"Maybe we could dress all serious or Goth, but then sing, like, a kids' song or an innocent song from the fifties," I proposed.

"Oh my *god,* that's fucking *amazing!*"

Penny suggested "Sugar, Sugar." "That stupid song is the worst! It's been stuck in my head for a month now."

"Sugar, du du du doo doo dooo, uh-huh, honey honey!" I sang. "Yeah, I mean, it doesn't show talent, but it would be hilarious. We should do it."

Penny laughed until her face turned red and tears squeezed out of her eyes. It was contagious. I started laughing too.

"We gotta." She started planning in between fits of laughter. "And a choreographed dance, all of us. Like the Charleston, the Jitterbug or something."

We laughed until we collapsed. I lay on the green, one hand in the dirt, the other pillowed on grass, still convulsed with merriment. Tara and Nicole had even more ideas.

"We'll throw candy at the audience. That'll win them over."

"And let's overdo it on the Goth, so when we get on stage, everyone thinks we'll be doing a weird interpretive dance to Bauhaus or the Sisters of Mercy. But no! We're sweet as candy—what a shock."

"Yes!" Still giggling but starting to calm down, I sat rubbing dirt from my hair. "It will be such a mind fuck. I can't wait to see how the audience reacts."

We won first prize. It was a rush being on stage, seeing the looks of disgust turn to delight and hilarity when we broke into song. I felt free. I was amazed at how my shyness melted away while on display. I loved wearing my borrowed clothes: fishnets and all black. I felt at home. After the performance, as we sat on the floor of Penny's and my dorm room, I kept checking out my reflection in the window. I needed to wear more black eye liner, I decided. And I definitely needed to actually spice up my wardrobe.

I started right away. On a day trip to Boston with my new friends, I was able to score a Marilyn Manson shirt.

At Camp Exploration, I got a heady taste of social acceptance and the freedom it brings. In Barre, I had to live the life of an introvert, either keeping to myself or hanging out with the few friends I clung to no matter how they disparaged me. But for those few summer weeks with camp friends, I was rewarded for expressing myself. I could be wild. I could be silly. I had actually played with fire in a limited way, throwing pieces of burning paper in the trash with a friend who shared my budding pyromania. I liked to see how big the flames could get before we'd have to put them out.

And then I had to return home with my new understanding that I actually love people and get along with them well, under the right conditions—which were lacking in Barre. I couldn't see any way to apply the summer's insights to my daily life at Spaulding. It felt like I'd been briefly sprung from jail, then locked up again.

CHAPTER 7

TRAMPINA

As soon as I learned that Goth style existed, I was drawn to it like a skull magnet to a black refrigerator.

I've always been attracted to the morbid things in life. Back on Long Island, when I was eight or nine, a friend and I illicitly entered a renovated garage on her family's property. We found candles and porno mags, dark sheets covering the windows. Not long after, the man who lived there but hadn't been home at the time committed a shocking act: he raped and murdered a jogger. My proximity to danger felt exciting to me. At this age, I made little distinction between real life and fiction. I gorged on scary flicks, along with a steady diet of books by R.L. Stine and Stephen King. When we moved to Vermont, I fantasized that our new house was haunted by a poltergeist and other angry spirits.

I still don't know where this fascination comes from; it's simply a part of me. My current job is writing true crime for *Oxygen,* which feeds my macabre curiosities on an almost daily basis. In my high school years, I mostly hid my interest in crime, instead expressing my "darkness" through my clothing and other aspects of Goth style— cutting included.

I saw some of the Goths I met at camp cut themselves, and I'd been doing it too, well before meeting them. When my mom noticed cuts on my wrists that I'd half-heartedly tried to hide with bracelets, she was horrified, wrongly assuming I'd tried to end my own life. It wasn't that, however, but an unhealthy response to stress. Some psychological studies have suggested that cutting releases mood-boosting endorphins. I believe that's what it did for me. Plus, I probably needed attention.

My first real glimpse of Goth style had come when I was still a freshman. My mom was teaching math at a school a few towns away from Barre, and I sat in on one of her classes. She was in remission then; her raven hair was growing back, but was still close to her head, the ringlets like the coat on a short-haired poodle. I fixated on one of the students, a girl a few years older than me. She had dyed her hair blue-black and adorned her eyes with a smoky black liner. Though her clothes were normal and I didn't know the word yet, I sensed the gothish vibe. I couldn't stop watching her; I wanted to be like that, and at the same time, I kind of hated her for having the guts to stand out from the crowd.

My mom said this girl was disturbed, that she was obsessed with dark imagery. I didn't forget her or the longing she inspired, and within months I was changing my own image accordingly. In my craving for a look that would match my interior, I felt an almost gravitational pull towards the Goth style and ethos.

Becoming friends with Tonya helped. Having bonded in French class over Marilyn Manson, we quickly formed a pivotal friendship. Sarah wasn't pleased, and aggressively tried to repel the brash girl with long legs who'd stepped into our little circle.

When Tonya ignored some jabs aimed at her for wearing pleather pants—Sarah called her a slut, despite the fact that none of us had even had our first kiss yet—the aggression escalated.

As we gathered around my locker before class, Sarah disparaged a sheer top I had on.

"I happen to like it," Tonya said. "I helped her pick it out."

That rebuttal really got under Sarah's freckled skin. I envied Tonya's gift for self-assertion, regretting that I didn't have her courage yet feeling fortunate to have her in my corner. Sarah's look said she was madly jealous of my blossoming friendship, and would strive to stunt the growth of that flower. After that, she tried being warmer with Tonya, possibly in an effort to turn the tables and arouse *my* jealousy. Tonya made it clear she wasn't interested. Her coldness was something Sarah wasn't used to.

A month after returning from Camp Exploration, I followed up on my quest to change my look by getting two chunky black streaks in my hair. They were midnight black, so black they were almost blue, and contrasted with highlights in the rest of my hair. I loved the way those streaks brought out my eyes, in tandem with black eyeliner. I caked so much sticky Maybelline "blackest black" mascara on my lashes that they looked like dead spider legs. My lips received a makeover, too; I often painted them a dark merlot red or eggplant purple. Sometimes I went full Goth and did them in black, using a pale powdered foundation for contrast on my face. My classmates reacted with a mix of wonder and disgust.

In the winter of my sophomore year, both Sarah and I made the Varsity cheerleading team. I proudly sewed my red, fuzzy letter, a big S, onto the back of my school jacket, by that point one of the few non-Goth clothing items I wore. My achievement was less impressive than it sounds. At Spaulding, cheerleading was a low prestige endeavor. The squad got referred to as heifers or cows because many members were considered overweight. I frequently wore my Goth-toned lipstick to cheerleading practice, and of course this annoyed my coach, as did the black streaks in my hair. She nagged me to hide those streaks during games and photo sessions. And she wasn't the only one to say similar things. My high school yearbooks are full of group photos in which I've tried to hide my streaks by tucking my hair behind my ears because teachers and other adults told me the look was too dramatic.

Despite not fitting in, I fucking loved cheerleading. The cheers themselves weren't the highlight; I had little school spirit left by this point. But I adored the stunts and dances. I especially loved being a top, getting thrown into the air, even though I mostly wasn't very skilled at it. Even when I did an okay job, my coach complained about my "weird" appearance. I just didn't have that cheerleader look, she'd say. So after that one season, I quit, concluding that I just wasn't wanted. It seemed like a repetition of what had happened when I tried to play sports in junior high.

One time, while we were out on the gymnasium floor performing a stunt with three girls high up in the air on one foot chanting "Go Big Red," a group of female basketball athletes (who were subjectively way more popular than us) showered packs of Big Red gum on us from the bleachers. One of the girls lost her balance and almost fell.   Still, there were a *few* popular girls on the team, one of which was the poor girl who could have gotten badly hurt during the Big Red incident.

Speaking of Big Red, by now after numerous incidents of numerous people being attacked by our vicious rooster, my parents decided to give him to my dad's coworker, a farmer. His farm was full of hens and roosters, and those roosters weren't impressed with Big Red's attitude upon his arrival. They ostracized him, and he ended up sleeping in a barn with cows until coyotes killed him one day. When I heard about how he died, alone and cast out, I felt sad.

I was beginning to know too much about rejection—not just the pain of not getting what I wanted, but the sting of having life withhold things I felt entitled to.

I was still pining for someone I hoped liked me back, but reality continued to slap me in the face. Unrequited love is painful enough in brief bursts, but this had dragged on for years. To make it worse, I nursed suspicions that my low social standing among my classmates was causing the person I obsessed about to deny his feelings for me.

I'd walk down the hallway, gripping one strap on my backpack and wondering if my walk was lopsided. My eyes clicked with Evan's as he stood by his locker. Heat flooded my cheeks; I looked away. The strength of my heartbeat shook me as I walked to my own locker. In my peripheral vision, I could still see him staring as I fumbled with my lock combination.

"Whatchou staring at that ugly girl for?" Evan's friend loudly whispered.

"That's not a nice thing to say,"he shot back, with assertion.

I smiled as I took out my history book. The fact that Evan was standing up for me was proof that he might like me. At the very least, it proved he respected me as a human being. And at this point in my life, that was pretty damn good.

In homeroom, I'd often feel him staring. Our desks were arranged in a horseshoe and his was across from me. When our eyes met, I'd have to look down. Sarah, sitting next to me, usually noticed. Once she wrote something in her notebook, ripped out the page and slid it over to me. It said, "That faggot is staring at you again. It's probably the cowlick in your hair."

The word "faggot" was all over our school, as it was in many places in the nineties, and Sarah often referred to Evan as such. (I used the word as well when describing straight people I didn't like, I hate to admit; we all did.) I shook my head in disapproval and crumpled up the note, then sat there patting my head to search for cowlicks.

As much as I liked Evan for treating me well—at least better than other boys did—I resented what I saw as his cowardice for possibly not admitting that he liked me back.

"I think I just have delusions, like how I think that Chinga deep down likes me. I think that a lot but IT'S A DELUSION GINA SO GET OVER IT," I wrote in my diary. I also sometimes wrote in my diary that I hated Evan. I had to fight the crush, to a certain extent at least; I felt like I was drowning when I got lost in visions of a connection that might indeed be delusional. When the pain got too bad, I cut myself to ease the intrusive thoughts. I also tried to date others, but those attempts came with their own kinds of humiliation and heartbreak.

I tried to date a tall, lanky boy named Todd, who was reasonably popular at Spaulding. He had icy blue eyes and white-blond caterpillar eyebrows. He liked rap music and his braces made me think of a white Lil' Wayne from the music video "#1 Stunna." He seemed to like me, though it was really hard to tell.

"We need to hang out," he proposed over the phone. He meant outside of school, where he would eye me and wink privately at me as we passed each other in the halls daily.

"Okay. Maybe J.J.'s Arcade?"

"Maybe. But we can't really make out there."

I was thrilled at this evidence that he really did like me, and shrugged it off when he made some remark about my "tramping around in those outfits."

"What outfits?" I asked, wrapping my fingers around the coils of the landline phone in my room.

"You know, like your leopard print skirt."

"Oh, I love that skirt." It certainly wasn't trampy. It almost came down to my knees. I thought it looked very rocker, very Shirley Manson-ish.

"And your dog collars," Todd added.

I said I liked them. And I did. I thought that Todd should like them, too but that thought seemed like a far-fetched fantasy.

The very next day, Evan complimented the dog collar around my neck. We were sitting next to each other in Spanish.

"I like your collar, it's badass," he said, pointing to the black leather band dotted with little spikes.

"Thanks," I said, my cheeks flushing. This was like a dream, but my body was in distress. I was overheating, starting to get woozy as he continued talking.

"I was in this mosh pit last summer in Massachusetts and this guy took one of those collars off his neck, wrapped it around his fist, and started punching people. Got me in the eye!"

Now I was really lost. Did he want me to laugh? Maybe I was supposed to say "ouch." Instead, I stared at my desk in confusion while pretending to write. For weeks afterwards, I regretted my inaction. What if he was trying to get something started? I might have blown my chances of even friendship with a boy who, unlike Todd, appreciated my style.

I told Sarah about my positive interaction with Evan and gushed, "this means he doesn't hate me."

She replied, "not necessarily."

She went on, "even if he did like you, it would only be to use you for sex. That's the energy you put out."

I frowned.

I wrote in my journal that night "Chinga is a nice guy. That is what I've liked him for so long and I could always see that he was." I also wrote that "you know how you can tell if someone hates you by their eyes? His look: doesn't hate me." I noted that despite my infatuation with him and realization that he likely liked me as a person, I failed to let my mind go too much further even though it did from time to time. I liked Todd, was attracted to him; I could talk to him in a way I could never talk to Evan. But it wasn't the same. I could only talk to Todd because I didn't really care as much.

I went out with Todd. We messed around. Sarah didn't approve. She said I was simply looking for attention and whoring myself out in the process.

"You did *what* with him? That's disgusting, Gina. Or should I say Trampina."

"I told you, I don't like that nickname."

She turned her back and gave me the silent treatment for a week after my hookup with Todd. Though we'd always had our conflicts, this was different. I felt isolated, more cut off from her than ever. At the same time, Todd was keeping his distance. He'd pass me in the halls without a look, let alone the smile or wink I used to get from him. As I soon found out, he was talking about me, furnishing plenty of gory (and exaggerated) details. He said I ripped off his belt like a porn star.

"I heard you're a real pro," one of his friends threw at me. Standing by my open locker, I ignored him. I zipped my velour jacket and shut the door.

"You're a freak *and* a freak," I heard as I walked away.

And even more humiliating, I heard him utter to one of his friends as I retreated that I "probably gave him a blow job with her nose, that thing's so big."

Still a virgin, I was deeply confused by being labeled as "slutty." I felt like I was behind the curve and had been punished immensely for trying to gain a little experience, for doing what I thought was normal. In my diary (the one with ELKA in black nail polish on the cover), I wrote of wanting to talk to my friends "about the Todd thing and how I feel I messed up." I noted that if I did, they only blamed me.

Not long after this, Todd got a real girlfriend. She was popular, wore fleece hoodies and tapered leg denim. The day I saw them holding hands in the hall, I went home from school and cried. Todd had made it perfectly clear where I stood: someone to be played with in secret, but not good enough to date officially.

"I'm so dumb," I whispered, sequestered in the bathroom. My brother was around and I didn't want him to see me cry. A sixth grader now, he had friends—even a girlfriend. I had to wonder what I was doing wrong if this kid who only a few years ago had been putting parmesan cheese in his hair was dating before his older sister.

Todd was the last boy I fooled around with—even so much as kissed—during my remaining time at Spaulding.

CHAPTER 8

ELKA'S NIGHTMARE

On April 16, 2007, 23-year-old Seung-Hui Cho, armed with two semi-automatic pistols, stormed the Virginia Tech Campus and fatally shot 32 people before killing himself. Cho had been enrolled in the institution, and in the wake of the massacre, the violent themes in some material he'd produced for writing classes caught the public eye, prompting a debate over the status of creative writing as a possible predictor of real world violence. His one act play *Richard McBeef* received particular scrutiny.

While anger clearly percolates throughout, the tone of this 10-page work is hardly diabolical.[6] Rather, it's juvenile and really pretty embarrassing. It starts off in the kitchen where 13-year-old John argues with his stepfather, Richard McBeef. In poorly constructed, exposition-heavy dialogue, the son hints that his stepdad killed his real dad and made it look like a boating accident. McBeef tries to molest John and the kid freaks out. Discovering this, the mother rails at Richard. "Are you a bisexual psycho rapist murderer! Please stop following me. Don't kill me," she implores.

Upstairs, John is screaming, "I hate him. Must kill Dick. Must kill Dick. Dick must die. Kill dick... Richard McBeef. What kind of name is that? What an asshole name. I don't like it. And look at his face. What an asshole face. I don't like his face at all. You don't think I can kill you, Dick? You don't think I can kill you?"

John attacks Richard with a chainsaw, but fails. Richard strikes the boy a fatal blow.

At the time of its composition, "Richard McBeef" disturbed one professor enough to go to the police. After the shooting, of course many indulged in classic post-mass-murder retrospection, suggesting that more ought to have been done. As is the case with so many shootings, school officials found themselves in an awkward spot: should they sound the alarm whenever someone writes anything disturbing, or opt for affirming creativity, even at the cost of possibly missing a warning sign?

It's a vexing question. More than one teen shooter has written stories about killing before committing horrific acts of violence. But what of all the kids who are fully capable of engaging emotionally and intellectually with fictional violence? Research has shown that their brains are ripe for processing darker stuff. And of course it's not just teens who are drawn to tales of death and mayhem. Plenty of "normal" people binge on shows about serial killers. Entire television networks focus on true crime, and their audience is primarily adult women. And in America, we are way more comfortable with being entertained by violence than peace. Nudity, just the human body in its natural form, is censored for television, while senseless savagery is not. One big problem with cracking down on teens' writing or other creative expression any time it makes adults uncomfortable is the risk that it will damage budding artists whose lurid imagery is anything but a literal forecast of homicide. My own experience in the nineties offers a case in point. I started writing to help me cope with my chaotic feelings, but also because it was just plain fun. I was such a prolific keeper of journals and diaries that by the time I graduated from Spaulding, they filled two sticker-covered lock boxes. I wrote many poems and absurdist horror stories, the latter partly inspired by all the horror films I watched. I'd been an avid fan since the long-ago days when my grandmother and I used to revel in *The Blob*.

I was also inspired by Shakespeare, that staple of English classes. Why shouldn't I be able to replicate his feat of composing a rhyming story with popular appeal? I came up with something I thought fit the bill. True, it wasn't as good—but I thought it was funnier.

The kernel came to me at the age of 14. One day I was doodling with the radio tuned to an FM station known for playing groups like Nine Inch Nails and Rob Zombie. Using a red pencil, I drew a pool of blood next to a pair of platform shoes. The caption read "Blood on the Dancefloor." A few days later I was watching MTV when Michael Jackson debuted a new song with that title.

I flipped out, sure it had to be some kind of sign. From there I grew obsessed with the image of a fictional massacre at a dance hall. I had dreams about it, nothing like a shooting, but a mix of *Scream* and Shakespearean tragedy. Guns? Boring, I thought, but kids getting killed by disco balls or being shoved off balconies—now that was interesting! It was one of my favorite fantasies to indulge while listening to music. I'd put on Garbage and spin scenarios in which I was the ultimate target. First, some of my classmates—the supporting characters—had to get bumped off in a range of unexpected ways. Finally the maniac would come after me, chasing me down the halls of the Elks Club until I locked myself in the bathroom.

And then I thought: what if *I* became a killer? Only because I was pushed too far, of course. I had to be a victim, but only up to a point. I had to write this story, but wasn't sure how. And then I realized that the key could be that memory I constantly returned to, the one that still caused me such confusion: the sixth grade dance at the Elks Club, when Evan stared at me while slow dancing with my friend. I didn't know why that moment stayed with me, I didn't want it to, but it was an obsession. I was gripped by the notion of discovering what it meant, because it *had* to mean something.

Despite those Shakespeare assignments, I knew almost nothing about the formal craft of poetry, but I decided that my book had to rhyme. Texts that rhymed seemed deeper, weightier—more important. That was my logic. As for the comic touches, I figured I could add inside jokes cooked up by my friends and me: a horny blue triangle named Trihornia; Bubbles, the rabid monkey; a man who'd try to flood the Elks Club by clogging the bathroom drains with wadded paper towels; another man who spent his time breaking clocks with rocks in an effort to literally halt time.

I began doodling scenes, assigning names. I took the moniker Elka for myself. Evan became Chinga, already his code name in the notes my friends and I passed in class. It came from a slip of the tongue my brother made, which I thought was even funnier when I discovered that the word means "fuck" in Mexican Spanish. At the same time, the sexual connotation made me blush. I could definitely picture making out with Evan, but anything more than that was out of my comfort zone. Our love was just too pure, I told myself.

I made up the word Glof for my villains. Principally, these were people whose names started with L, M, or N. (I was thinking of several junior high friends I was no longer close with.) I even put together a "Glof Chart" to pin down the story's epicenter of evil. Its formula equated specific letters of the alphabet with percentages of "gloffiness," from L, M, and N at 100% to F and T at 1.5625%.

This chart would later be misconstrued as a kill list. It didn't help that my circle and I formed the habit of cursing the "damn glofs" when we got mad — especially if the offenders' names happened to start with L, M, or N.

I gave Sarah the unglamorous nickname Shuffles. Tonya was Anya, an Eastern European-sounding name that I liked because it seemed akin to Elka, reflecting my sense that we were on the same wavelength. I grew increasingly obsessed with this story while writing it and embarrassingly so. All my binders were covered in quotes from it. A photograph of me shows me proudly holding up a painting I made of a disco ball above a school hallway that was running with blood, not unlike (and probably inspired by) the blood waves rushing from the elevators of *The Shining*. The amusement of the story wasn't just contained in my own teenage mind.

The minute I had an outline, even before I started writing, I began talking it up to my small group of friends. Once I had actual pages, I shared them, and soon enough we were all quoting from it. Sarah and I especially enjoyed reciting the following passage:

"I can't believe what happened to your eye.
It's the same thing that happened to that guy!"

Shuffles said, "shut the fuck up Elka, you freak,
it's the same thing that happened to that geek.
Steve is his name, him and Stuart were playing chess,
Stuart got excited and oh, what a mess!
He knocked Steve in the eye with a black wooden pawn,
leaving him unconscious on his own front lawn."

We also loved to sing an introductory song that I'd made up and shared early on:

Many, many years ago in 1993,

I began to like this lanky kid but he did not like me.

Someone gloffy asked him out for me and he said maybe.

I don't know what happened then, it all got screwy.

I forgot about what happened for quite some time

Then came the Elks Club dance and oops, never mind.

I would like to explain it but the words are hard to find

About that disturbing dance in March that fucked up my mind.

Honestly, the idea for the song came from Tom Arnold performing "I'm My Own Grandpa" in the 1996 movie *The Stupids*. I watched a clip of him in a straw boater hat singing the rhyming diddy which begins with the line "Many, many years ago when I was 23." I saw this performance just once on HBO at Sarah's home and it, embarrassingly, kicked off a series of events that ultimately ruined my life for a while. And why did we find this diddy *so* hilarious? I don't know. The sixth grade dance was hardly earth-shattering enough to warrant a mini-epic on the subject. On the other hand, what else would I be doing? At fourteen and fifteen, I didn't have a cell phone. We still had dial-up internet. Mom would only let me log on for one-hour sessions because she didn't want to tie up the phone line. What if there was an emergency and someone tried to call? The most exciting thing my friends and I did was go to the movies. My peers who had cars cruised around downtown Barre and got wasted in fields. I would have joined in, doing drugs or getting drunk in cow pastures, but I wasn't invited.

I began to like the fact that my jokes and writing affected others. It wasn't a big influence, but I could make people laugh. Without much effort, I could create jokes that got picked up and spread, at least within a small group. Before long, my friends were exchanging notes sprinkled with Elks Club references and jokes about sixth grade and allusions to the characters in my story. Even Scary Barre, my rhyming nickname for our town, seemed to take off.

It started to seem like I had some charisma. Not major charisma, of course; not serial killer charisma. Not even cult leader charisma. Just enough that I thought that maybe, someday, I could make friends in the absence of Sarah. And when I thought back to my experience at Camp Exploration, it stoked a rage that my writing could feed on. I'd listen to Lesley Gore's "You Don't Own Me" and think of the ways that Sarah had treated me like her doll. I finally understood that it actually wasn't normal to be bossed, to be constantly at the mercy of your controlling "best friend."

I wanted to get out from under all that, and yet I couldn't face the break. Sarah didn't want us to be separated, ever. After Spaulding, we were planning to attend the same college. Would things still feel so toxic later on, or maybe chill out once we found our respective husbands?

I decided that I had to finish my book by March 25, 1998, the same date (though not the same year—the story is set in 1994) on which the action takes place. I christened that date Glof Day. Tonya and I would joke about it. I still have a poster-sized drawing she gave me honoring this "holiday."

Writing about the Elks Club gave the place more meaning than it used to have for me. When I rode past in the back seat of Mom's Toyota Camry, I'd peer at the building, trying to get a glimpse of the interior through the windows. I couldn't see the balcony, but I remembered what it looked like and figured it would be the perfect setting for my climax. This was where my 11-year-olds would fight, a bunch of mean girls trying to push each other off.

I dragged a cork board up from our basement, imagining I could keep track of the details of my story the way FBI agents track serial killers in movies. There'd be pictures and lists and thumb tacks and strings, and it would look neat and begin to make sense. But I kept getting more and more ideas, which I crowded onto a sheet of lined paper. Soon both sides were covered with a mish-mosh of scrawls, spiral drawings, and miniature pyramids of thoughts.

My choice of title was straightforward: *Elka's Nightmare at the Elks Lodge.* I picked a Halloween font, chunky letters with dripping blood. I discovered, via an exhaustive internet search, that a band called the Swirling Eddies had written a song with that name, and figured it had to have a message just for me—something as dark and deep as the tale I hoped to write. But I couldn't find a recording at the time. When, years later, I finally tracked it down, I was crestfallen to learn it was actually jam band music.

Writing the first few chapters was easy, but halfway through I was flagging. In particular, I struggled with my own rule that it had to rhyme throughout. I wrote the ending before completing large chunks of the middle. It climaxes with me (in the guise of Elka) accidentally killing Evan (Chinga) in my effort to murder the girl he is dancing with to "Stairway to Heaven," a song that has probably prompted a lot of kids to want to commit homicide. I then chase her up to the famous balcony. We struggle and I push her over the edge—but not before she cuts the string to the disco ball, which falls, killing four others. Then I stab myself with a flag pole and die.

Prior to this climax, I inserted a few other random murders: the revenge stabbing by 12-year-old Koby of her boyfriend and a classmate; the kidnapping of an 11-year-old girl (with implied intent to kill) by a male adult named Boomer; and the deaths of top hat-wearing Mr. Chips, a panicky janitor named Rodney, and plenty of glofs.

When my "book" was finally finished, I showed it to my mom. Naturally, I hoped she would praise my creation. Having spent months putting flesh on the bones of my idea, I saw the result as my major literary achievement to date.

She handed the manuscript back without a word.

"What did you think?" I stood in her bedroom doorway, watching her fold blue and gray bathroom towels.

"It's disturbing," she said. She was facing away from me. I could see how tightly her jeans fit her legs. She'd gained about ten pounds, which she blamed on the chemo.

"What, why?"

"You shouldn't be having those kinds of thoughts at this age."

"What do you mean, it's all pretend."

"But it's based on some truth, Gina. I know that."

"Does that mean Stephen King is disturbing too?"

"Don't be a smartass, Gina."

I rolled my eyes. I took my manuscript — a pile of papers stapled together — and went up to my room. I sat on my bed and flipped to a random passage:

Never trust a smiling blue triangle with gloves. That is what my Koby said.

Koby, the lovable religious girl who enjoys Skittles and has hair the color of red.

I chuckled. It was so funny to me. My mom was wrong. It's not disturbing, it's *funny.*

Throughout my teen journals, I doodled, *"take the a off my name and add an s, that spells the place of my death.* — *Elka*

CHAPTER 9

YOU DON'T OWN ME

As junior year began, I was bolder than before, but only with my clothing. If I couldn't stand up for myself in verbal exchanges, I could through my outfits, which now ran to spikes and fishnets, extra short skirts, even a corset. No longer the child who fancied bright bows and tropical fish shorts, I'd become a major fan of all black.

My new look wasn't received well at Spaulding, a fact that made me more and more aggrieved. Acquaintances stopped wanting to be seen in my company. Some of their parents told them I'd turned "evil." Every day I endured a barrage of insults: "freak," "slut," "weirdo," and my personal favorite, "Satanist." Evan, I noticed, was dressing funkier too: vintage tees, pleather shirts, button-ups with a dragon pattern. It drew me to him even more, but I did have to wonder why *his* unconventional wardrobe (admittedly not goth-leaning) didn't turn him into an outcast the way mine did.

Sarah roundly disapproved of my rebellion through clothing, and boy, did she let me know it. Every day I heard what an attention whore I was, what a slut, what a freak. That I had no self-respect. That I'd only attract shithead guys.

One day I walked into English class feeling good about my outfit. I was wearing a new plaid dress with safety pins for decorations. I sat down at my desk behind Sarah. She pivoted and looked me up and down.

"What the fuck are you wearing? I mean, that skirt could be kinda nice if it wasn't so short."

I looked down at myself. The skirt *was* short, but I thought it looked badass. Suddenly scared I was flashing my underwear, I crossed my legs in their metallic fishnets.

"Where did you buy all that? Definitely didn't come from around here."

Sarah was on to me. I couldn't lie. "I went shopping in New Hampshire. At the mall in Salem. With Tonya and her mom."

Turning away, she sucked in her breath. "And you didn't tell me." Her voice was soft, eyes focused on the blackboard.

"I'm sorry," I said. If she hated anything more than self-determined style, it was my bond with Tonya.

Our classmates arrived. As one of them passed me, an overweight, baby-faced boy in a camo shirt and cargo pants snapped the fake tattoo choker I wore on my upper arm.

"What the hell is this? This chick wears the *weirdest* things."

"Idiot," I said sotto voce, while Sarah chuckled at his comment.

Our teacher Mrs. Reardon, a woman in her fifties who I thought dressed like something out of Puritan Boston, told us to take out our homework, which concerned *The Scarlet Letter.* She called on Sarah.

"I think that Hester Prynne brought on her own punishment," Sarah read out clearly and loudly. "She needed to take more responsibility for her actions and think before she acted."

This, I thought, was a classic Sarah move. She really embodied that old school Puritan vibe. I began zoning out and started drawing my name in bubble text on my own homework sheet.

In the reading journal that we had to keep, periodically reviewed by Mrs. Reardon, I reflected on what struck me as Hawthorne's commentary on the human tendency to label other people. "I think that maybe it was alright for Hester to be punished but not forever. Her daughter Pearl was a constant reminder. The A was a reminder of her sin for her whole life and the gravestone was a reminder for all of Hester's eternity. She could never escape from her 'mistake' she made and I think it is wrong to be punished forever."

I got back Mrs. Reardon's comment: "Excellent, thanks, Gina! You've made my day!"

Meanwhile, I felt like I had been stamped with an invisible scarlet "O" for Outsider. The jacket I used to wear, with the Varsity "S" on the back, was buried deep in my closet, unworn and unloved.

My hurt was compounded when my old teacher Ms. Scharf—the one from PSTL in junior high—turned up in the hall at Spaulding. Excited, I waved to her, but she walked right past me. I decided maybe she didn't recognize me, but Sarah said she definitely did. "She emailed me. She's started teaching in the vo-tech center. She asked what was wrong with you."

"What do you mean, wrong?"

"Your clothes."

It was a shock. Mrs. Scharf had been my mentor. I looked up to her. She'd pushed me to do my best. She was liberal, a proponent of the arts. I'd assumed she truly championed self-expression.

"But I wasn't even dressed that freaky today." Just the dog collar and the copious eye liner, topping a pink tee and denim jeans.

Sarah laughed. "I told her you lost your mind." She babbled on, calling Tonya a bitch. She really couldn't stand my growing closeness to a friend with whom I could be my full silly self. When I turned sixteen, Tonya wrote on my birthday card, "Dear Elka, I hope you like the gift. Happy B-day! Love, Tonya." The name Tonya was crossed off. Above it, a box said "deceased," and she'd signed again: "Anya."

In my diary, I wrote about Sarah's "wicked mean" behavior. "She is always telling people I deserve to be punished and that I'm obsessive and stupid. Why do I put up with this?"

I may not have been stupid or deserving of punishment, but I was definitely obsessive. It had gotten to the point where I'd repeat in my head the parting words of a social interaction; then I'd write down a line for every syllable in those words. The ritual helped me stop going over what had happened as I anxiously wondered if I'd said something dumb. I think I got a similar benefit from indulging in repetitive jokes of the sort that figured so heavily in *Elka's Nightmare,* and while this offered a more constructive outlet than washing my hands a million times a day, it got me into trouble all the same.

I started doodling in my journal pictures of me at Junior Prom, wearing a black dress with matching faux feather trim. Impaled on a flagpole, I stand smiling, alone on the dance floor. The flag is an Elks Club flag, the image echoing the absurd and bloody climax of my book.

I wrote about needing to find a dress for prom, one fit to mark a uniquely memorable occasion. Where I used to spin stories about our house being haunted by a poltergeist, I now reveled in dark fantasies that something crazy would happen on prom night—not caused by me, and not involving any deaths, but something exciting and supernatural.

I couldn't help but think that Brenda Spencer looked badass. She was just sixteen when she shot up an elementary school across from her home, killing the principal and a custodian in addition to wounding eight children and a cop. This had happened in the 1970s; the Boomtown Rats later wrote a song about it, entitled "I Don't Like Mondays," based on Brenda's reply when asked why she did it: "I don't like Mondays. This livens up the days."

One week before the shooting, she reportedly told a classmate that she was planning to do something big to get on television. She'd had previous brushes with the law involving theft and vandalism, and harbored fantasies of becoming a sniper. When I researched her story, I lingered on her photo. She was lean and lanky with stringy red hair. Opaque rose-colored Jeffrey Dahmer-esque glasses swallowed her freckled face. I was attracted to that Manson Family look.

I'm not proud of that thought. I didn't like what she did. I assumed I could never hurt another person. When I clash with someone I don't want them dead, just out of my life. That's how I feel now, and at bottom I wasn't all that different, even back in my high school days. I asked myself then, and still do: would I have felt as attracted to Brenda's badass vibe if I'd never heard a song inspired by her actions? Maybe I was influenced by the fact that some people thought I could be just like her—a perception, however repulsive, that granted power to its object. The image of the outlaw or renegade appealed to me more and more as I felt myself being pushed away by my peers.

Well before the rumors of my homicidal bent began to circulate, I was a prime target of gossip. The source was usually Sarah, as happened on the occasion when she spread mean stories about Todd and me. Over the summer, she made up the tale that I'd taken acid in sixth grade and hallucinated blue triangles trying to rape me. She told it to Evan over AOL chat, then shared the chat with me. "It really fucked her up," she told him. "That's why she's all psycho and gothic now." She also told a number of people that Tonya and I were "lesbian lovers," meanwhile continuing to broadcast that I was slutty, that I slept around and had no respect for myself. Sometimes I'd express that I didn't like this, but other times I reacted with cowardice, scared that any talk-back would result in more abuse.

After all this, the next development still caught me off guard. Sarah approached as I stood in front of my locker, wildfire in her eyes. Silently, she handed me a note. I opened my mouth but she was already off. As she headed down the hall, I saw her right arm rise in the familiar gesture of flipping her shoulder-length hair. I looked down. The note was folded like a football, with "For your eyes only" written on the outside. I scanned its four pages, written in purple gel pen. She rehashed her criticisms of my wardrobe, my tendency to smoke cigarettes from time to time, and my hookup with Todd, accusing me of a failure of self-respect. "Dressing like a prostitute won't get you a good boyfriend... And don't even get me started on Tonya. She won't have to worry about being a slut because guys don't want to date anal-retentive women. Despite that she sure as fuck dresses like a whore.

"Gina, you've changed. Changed into something I don't want to be around."

Declaring she'd be better off without me, she went on to claim that she had found a new best friend in Donna, a buddy of ours. Despite what she said, I got the feeling that she hoped I'd run after her with an apology. Instead, I felt relieved. I stuffed the note into my backpack and headed off to class, planning to avoid her for the rest of the day. I had long wanted to end our friendship but feared that her retaliation would be far worse than remaining friends. Now it felt as though the hard part was completed by her. And, maybe, there would be no retaliation?

"I don't know why I put up with her shit for so long," I told Tonya as she drove me home after school. By now, she was in the habit of doing that every day. I had a definite feeling that change was in store for me. I hoped for something positive.

"We should totally shaving cream Sarah's car," Tonya said. "Mrs. 'I can dish it out but I can't take it.' Maybe *she* should get something bad."

I liked that idea.

That night, I read the note again. Sarah claimed that her new best friend had helped with the writing, but the font and voice were unmistakably her own. Donna didn't even sign her name, but I knew she would follow Sarah's lead. All the stuff about my clothing really drove me up the wall. Who wants to "dress like a grownup" when they are still a teen? I felt like she was attacking a precious method of self-expression, one that it had taken me years to arrive at.

"Thank fucking God," I said to myself. "I'm finally free." I closed my eyes and pictured Sarah's tan car slathered with shaving cream and raw eggs. The word "bitch" was written in puffy white letters. Egg yolk dripped from the driver's door handle. I chuckled, then opened my journal and wrote my review of Sarah's note and behavior. "*I* wouldn't ditch a friend even if she/he was a drug addict. I'd just try to help them, but I wouldn't harass them and put them down... True friends let their friends live their lives! Sarah is not my mom!... Tonya is a much better friend. She doesn't put me down."

The next day, Tonya blared Marilyn Manson's "Cryptorchid," a track from Antichrist Superstar, as we sped toward school. Approaching, we could see the school through the trees. A cloud of smoke hovered over the grubs' gathering spot.

She slowed her Grand Am car and dawdled past the student parking lot. "I don't want to go to school today."

"Me either."

"Fuck it, then." The car picked up speed. Tonya boosted the volume on Marilyn Manson. She had the windows open, and the wind whipped our hair, the black and blond strands all over my face as I tried to tuck them behind my ears. The air was cool, the sky still a little bit dark.

"Wanna drive up to Burlington?" she asked.

"Yeah!" It felt like the perfect thing to do. I thought of Burlington as being like a real city—or at least the closest thing you'd find in Vermont. We could shop, hang out at a cafe, meet interesting people. Maybe some cute boys. Maybe one with a blue mohawk who dressed kinda punk and would ask me for my number.

On I-89, we saw a dark green van. Tonya, zipping along, was on the verge of passing it when I spotted the dent in its bumper.

"Oh shit," I said. That's my dad."

She eased up on the gas and moved back into the right-hand lane, then pulled off at the next exit, Waterbury. We stopped at a gas station for Mountain Dews.

"That was close. I don't know where he was going. He doesn't work up north."

The rest of the drive was blessedly parent-free. It was still early enough in the morning that white puffs of fog hugged the mountain terrain, clinging in green crevices beneath snow-covered heights.

Tonya switched the music to the "All in the Family" track from her KoRn CD. Two adult men slung homophobic insults in a pseudo-rap/rock musical battle.

"This song is so stupid," she said.

"I know." I fussed with a tear in my red fishnet stockings. The pointy ring on my right index finger kept snagging on them.

Hanging out with Tonya felt so easy. Conversation flowed smoothly, free of hostility. I relaxed in the absence of critical eyes.

In Burlington, we parked in a lot. The city seemed quiet.

"Is anything gonna be open?" Tonya asked. We'd driven so fast, it was still just a few minutes after eight a.m.

I shivered, hands in my pockets. I hadn't thought of that. We walked slowly around the empty streets, not at all as I'd pictured. After our second circuit of the downtown business district plus a thorough examination of pedestrian-only Church Street, we once again came to Mr. Mike's pizzeria, a restaurant near the parking lot where we'd left the Grand Am.

"Hey, look," I said. A fire truck, lights flashing, though minus the siren, was pulling into the lot. A cop car was parked, and the cop stood next to it. He was writing something.

"Oh, God. My car," Tonya said.

The car had rolled backwards, hit a BMW. Of all the possible victims, it had to be an expensive one.

"Fuck! Must've forgotten the damn emergency brake."

Approaching, we were welcomed by a firefighter.

"The damaged car belongs to Mr. Mike. He's not in the pizzeria, but we'll take your information and get it to him later."

While initially shaken by the incident, Tonya put on Insane Clown Posse's "Bugz on my Nutz," a catchy, and in retrospect deeply sexist, song about contracting scabies. We were soon laughing at the absurdity of the lyrics, as we often did. Being in Tonya's presence felt light and easy.

By the time Tonya got back home, Mr. Mike had left a message on her family's answering machine. Tonya's mother grounded her. I got grounded, too. Mom said that my dad's coworker had spotted us on the road, but I later learned she had another information source: she was sneaking into my night table drawer and reading my journal. She tried to blame it on my brother, but later confessed. She felt bad and bought me a lock box so I could have some privacy.

What could I do while grounded? Play with a new toy, my favorite possession at the time: an Aiwa micro-cassette tape recorder. I liked to record myself making weird voices, then speed them up or slow them down for comical effect. One of the recordings I made at that time featuring church music from the TGN channel; over it, I'm yelling, "No, not my Jimmy! My beautiful son!" When I rewound it and played it at a slower speed, I was in tears, I was laughing so hard. I thought it was so funny, the chaotic scene I pictured: a grieving father freaking out at his son's funeral, fighting with someone, and knocking over the coffin à la *Pet Semetary*. The next day, I played Tonya the recording in the locker room before gym class and we giggled. We quoted it for days.

I figured that Tonya and I were only situational outcasts; it wasn't our choice, or our fault. I thought that we were interesting people who wanted to explore life to the best of our ability, but were thwarted by our social position in high school. Without Sarah and our old group of friends, it was just us two. We were barely invited to even the nerdiest of parties. We weren't included in anything.

Tonya and I didn't drink or do drugs, although we did smoke cigarettes. I always felt that our sobriety was simply because we didn't have access to any fun substances. On the weekends we'd drive around like maniacs, screeching the tires on Tonya's car as we circled a granite quarry. We'd swing by the video rental and rent two or three movies. Next we'd hit the Price Chopper, where we spent most of our time when we weren't either at home or in school, and stock up on junk food. I could eat an entire tub of vanilla frosting, spooning it up while I sat on Tonya's couch. I loved it at her place because I could get away with so many things that were forbidden in my house. Not really bad things, just dopey teen types of things. My mom, for instance, wouldn't let us drink soda, except once in a while when we got to order a pizza. My brother and I looked forward to this for days. It seemed like ours was the only house in Barre where a bottle of Coca-Cola was a luxury item. At Tonya's, soda was always available; in fact, her family consumed it as a water substitute. Her parents walked around with bottles of Mountain Dew in hand. It felt good to break my family's law by refreshing myself with neon green corn syrup, a beverage that resembled engine coolant. I knew that Mom's cancer made her extra cautious about what was going into her kids' insides; she didn't want us to get sick. I rebelled against her care.

Tonya and I loved to get lost in our own dorky world. We'd talk in weird voices, quoting my Elks Club book and coming up with more and more inside jokes. We started skipping school frequently, forging notes from our parents to get us excused, but our days off never matched the excitement of that day we drove to Burlington. We'd sit in Tonya's car in the Price Chopper parking lot, listening to CDs and drinking soda, smoking cigarettes and drawing in our notebooks for hours. We were bored, but it was a hell of a lot better than subjecting ourselves to all the bullying at Spaulding. Meanwhile, I was looking forward to passing my Driver's Ed test so I too could whiz around town. Though I felt my teacher had something against me. Around this time, I wrote in my journal, "I failed my driving test today again because my driving teacher is an asshole and he hates me because I'm a flatlander who wasn't born in Vermont."

I felt more and more justified in my hatred of school, having witnessed some of my peers' despicable behavior when an unpopular classmate died. I saw kids mocking other kids who'd lost their friend, openly laughing at them for crying.

I wrote, "Yesterday a freshman from SHS died in a car accident. He took out his parents' van. He hangs out with Dan and all the grubs. You know what really pisses me off about Spaulding High School... No one cares!! Just because the kid wasn't popular no one cared especially the teachers. The teachers only love the kids with popular names in the town. They didn't even announce it [his death] in the loudspeaker which is so mean. Because they usually do when someone dies. Popularity shouldn't matter when you die. It's supposed to be tragic. No one would care if I died. They'd laugh like they do when others die. [...] Heartless school."

It wasn't the first time I noticed the unfairness when a classmate died. A few months earlier, another unpopular teen died after a long battle with cancer. I overheard my peer, a boy say something disgusting: "Did you hear that that faggot finally died?" I was walking down a partially stairwell, behind him and his friend. They laughed. That moment secured what I already assumed: that nobody would care if people of my social stature died.

I took such episodes very personally, as confirmation of something I already assumed: outcasts like me could die and people wouldn't care.

We were nothing. We were garbage.

Being treated like garbage made me really vulnerable. I felt like I wasn't part of society, and that my only real peers were outliers and criminals, old poets who lived in remote shacks in the woods, and misunderstood murderers. The memory of that feeling gives me a certain insight into the kinds of people who express sympathy for shocking acts of mass murder. To the consternation of many, figures like the Columbine High School shooters and Elliot Rodger, perpetrator of the 2014 Isla Vista massacre, gain thousands of anonymous and even public sympathizers. There's no doubt in my mind that some of these people are reacting to the pain of social rejection—a sense that in the eyes of others, and therefore their own, they're no longer quite human; and perhaps no longer feeling human allows them to also dehumanize their victims. That doesn't make their thinking right, or even excusable, but it does make sense.

CHAPTER 10

COLUMBINE

April 20, 1999: it was spring break. I slouched on the rug in my bedroom watching MTV: white kids dancing on the sand in Cancún, Mexico. Teal waves crashed behind the featured boy band flanked by frenetic crowds of young women in bikinis and young men in baggy swim trunks, their baseball caps on backwards. I eyed them with disdain.

"There's been a shooting at a school," my mom said, poking her head through the doorway where I'd hung a beaded curtain from the Alloy catalog: blue and pink beads with an image of the Buddha. "It looks pretty bad," she added.

"Oh really?" I asked, but without enthusiasm. Languidly I pointed the remote at the boxy television set and switched to CBS, where the breaking news had pre-empted regular programming. I saw a kid fall out of a broken window in a shower of glass, and learned that it was happening at a high school in Colorado.

Immediately alert, I sat up, intent on the aerial shots of kids running out of the school, their arms flailing to the whirring of helicopters. I had never seen anything like it. Being on vacation heightened my interest; I had more free time to focus on it.

Tips and dubious claims rolled in and got relayed to the public by various newscasters. "It's being reported that the killers listened to Marilyn Manson," one of them said.

Other news outlets speculated that there might have been more than two shooters. Three black-clad teens were shown being arrested, prompting rumors of co-conspirator—possibly a third shooter on the roof. Although some still cling to that theory today, all three teens were later cleared, and all shots fired in the Columbine High School massacre have been accounted for.

One witness, a brown-haired girl with a silver barbell eyebrow ring, sobbed as she told a reporter that one of the shooters said "it was all because people were mean to him last year."

Oh wow, I thought. Sounds like maybe they were bullied.

Another witness claimed they belonged to "the Trench Coat Mafia," a supposed "Goth gang" that "wore long coats and kept to themselves."

"I don't think *Goth gangs* exist," I told the TV. These newscasters were old. Of course they didn't get it.

I flipped the channel. An anchor asked an expert whether Goth music could have played a role in the tragedy.

"Singers like Marilyn Manson advocate hate. They do encourage teen violence—so, yes, it's possible."

"Gina, time for dinner!" Mom hollered from downstairs.

"Just a minute." I flipped to another channel, unwilling to turn away despite my irritation with people who so clearly didn't know what they were talking about.

"They were outcasts. They were losers. They didn't belong," said a teen in a varsity jacket.

The screen flashed to images of Eric Harris and Dylan Klebold: grainy, black and white school photos of two generic young men. They didn't look Goth. They weren't wearing black. In fact, they seemed pretty run of the mill. And yet, the reporting made them sound like *me*. They liked my kind of music and they didn't fit in. Imagining I knew the kinds of torments they'd endured, I soon decided they must have just snapped.

The next day, I saw an interview with a Columbine student named Tiffany who said she'd been in a class with Eric and had gone to homecoming with him. He wanted to keep on dating, but she wasn't interested. Either in retaliation or hoping to win her back (or possibly both), he faked his death in front of her, pouring fake blood all over himself and lying on the ground. I thought of the time I'd used dental tablets to pretend I was injured. Tiffany said that Eric had inscribed "Ich bin Gott" ("I am God") in her yearbook. That stuck with me; I thought it was cool, and I figured he was hurt that she'd rejected him. I could relate to that.

I heard my own father call Eric and Dylan monsters, a term that was popular in the media. What a rigid outlook that reflected, I thought. These guys aren't monsters, they were just pushed too far. The people who reach for these labels are just too scared to admit that all of us are capable of just about anything. Four days after the shooting, I wrote in my journal, "The massacre in Littleton, well it's really annoying how they are blaming it all on Manson and now every channel's talking about how troubled Goths are. Lots of people are trying to imitate Eric Harris and his friend. On AOL, so many people worship the Trench Coat Mafia. I can understand though. They were victims too. I can totally relate. And actions like this are the only things that speak out. I'm not saying that killing is right but the media shouldn't keep exaggerating and bashing a subculture they know nothing about. I don't think I'm that Goth. I do dress Goth sometimes and listen to Goth music and I'm considered it. So, therefore it offends me that they say this shit."

The influence of Columbine began infiltrating my dreams nearly immediately. Just two days after the shooting, I had a dream that I was shot inside Spaulding, by my old sixth grade friend no less.

"I went to school and Nadine shot me in the shoulder and I laid down until she left. I called my mom and she didn't care I was shot. It healed up."

Later, I would cut out and annotate in my scrapbook a *Time* magazine article that quoted a football player named Evan Todd who was wounded in the school library. Evan maintained that Columbine was "a clean, good place except for these rejects [Klebold and Harris]... They were into witchcraft. They were into voodoo dolls. Sure, we teased them. But what do you expect with kids who come to school with weird hairdos and horns on their hats? ... They're a bunch of homos."

I was outraged that the article seemed to treat this anti-gay sentiment as normal, that it downplayed the harassment of those who were different. *"Fuck Evan Todd,"* I wrote on the clipping, next to a series of question marks in different colored pens. *"Why is this acceptable?! The media seems to think so.... Too bad Todd wasn't killed instead of one of the nicer kids like Rachel?"* (I was referencing Columbine victim Rachel Scott, who by all media accounts I had absorbed would likely never bully anyone.)

In the wake of the massacre, the term "Trench Coat Mafia" became a household phrase throughout the U.S. and beyond. The BBC reported[7] that "Children who survived the shooting spree say the two dead killers, both of whom wore ski masks and trench coats, were members of a close-knit group of 'loners' known as the 'trench coat mafia.' This group—which had an entry in the school's 1998 yearbook—is variously described as being obsessed with guns, Nazis, the military, the Internet, rock singer Marilyn Manson and Goth-rock culture." The report acknowledged, however, that Eric Harris and Dylan Klebold did not appear in a 1998 yearbook photo of the group. It later emerged that this was because they were only loosely connected to the clique, a "nonviolent school group of computer gamers established a few years before the shooting," in the words of journalist David Cullen[8], who wrote a book on Columbine.

I was far from the only one transfixed by the wall to wall coverage, obsessively watching CNN for updates. A *New York Magazine* writer[9] noted that his two daughters, one a pre-teen and the other a teenager, "can't get enough. They eat dinner in front of the set, fearful they will miss a single recap. In a tangential, contained way, it's like when Kennedy was shot and another crop of teenagers listened to Chet Huntley and Walter Cronkite intone those same things about Oswald and Ruby a thousand times until they became ritual knowledge." He said that his Goth teen daughter's "first reaction was to be pissed that the media creeps had assigned the Trench Coat Mafia to her chosen fashion bag."

In 2003, Glenn Muschert, a Purdue University professor specializing in mass media coverage of high profile crimes, released a study that concluding that the media response to Columbine incited an irrational level of fear, as "the nation became terrified that our schools were no longer safe, even though the facts show they are safer than ever."[10]Having sifted through more than 700 broadcast media transcripts and print articles that aired or were published in the month after the shooting, Muschert noted the persistence of heavy coverage whose slant he believed contributed to an exaggerated sense of danger. "The media focused on the cause of the shootings, and how people from Littleton, as well as people far removed from the Colorado area, reacted. Devoting so much coverage to reactions conveys the message that the reasons for the shootings were more important than the shootings. The search for meaning then became a priority for people throughout the country so they could apply that information to their schools and communities."

If it's true that the way the Columbine story was covered made people in far-flung locales feel as though the tragedy had occurred in their own backyards, it makes sense that many of them would seize on details of the event (such as the purported Goth connection) in an effort to predict and thwart the next attack. But, as my experience shows, it was perfectly possible to react to the intense coverage with a very different response. For me, it engendered sympathy for Harris and Klebold. I felt empowered by the prospect that their actions could frighten bullies enough to force a change in their behavior. I wondered what Sarah thought, if she'd been chastened by Columbine.

The fact is that partly thanks to how it was covered— the bloodbath of April 20, 1999 became far more than a self-contained tragedy. Glenn Muschert's conclusions about exaggerated fears around school safety notwithstanding, it did fuel a great deal of subsequent hate and carnage. At the same time, I believe it gave rise to a damaging level of misunderstanding and negative judgment directed at kids perceived to be "other."

In 2017, I interviewed Special Agent Michelle Lee[11], media coordinator for the San Antonio FBI, about how people respond to mass murder coverage and whether it encourages copycat crimes. She told me that the Bureau has observed "many potential attackers [who] express a *contextually inappropriate* interest—or in some cases a fixation—on past attacks and attackers. For instance, Columbine remains a frequently cited event by many attackers who seek to emulate the shooters and eclipse the number of victims." A 2014 report cited 17 attacks that were clearly inspired by it, in addition to dozens of plots and serious threats with a similar connection. In 2014, for instance, a 26-year-old man shot up Seattle University, killing one and injuring two others. He named Eric Harris as one of his idols.

Why, even after so many years have passed—years that have seen far deadlier mass shootings—does Columbine continue to exert such fascination? Does it have something to do with the saturation coverage, the way that newscasters harped on pinpointing causes throughout a 24-hour news cycle that the public wasn't used to at that time? Did experiencing that stamp the American psyche in some indelible way?

As I've said, it certainly made its mark on me. And to some extent, though I wasn't a killer and had no intention of committing physical violence, it inspired me to act. Soon Tonya and I would be swept up in the sick wave of kids making copycat threats. The fact that we were mere droplets of water in that tsunami didn't spare us, our perceived enemies, or the small town of Barre from the damaging consequences.

CHAPTER 11

LIKE ERIC HARRIS ON A MINOR LEVEL

Despite my naive and twisted hope, Columbine did not seem to deter Sarah's bullying. And even though she initiated our friendship breakup, she continued behaving like a jilted and rejected lover. She'd send me numerous emails to my AOL account, many of which referred to my behavior as slutty and my clothing as inappropriate. She was angry, and deeply hurt, that I wasn't trying to get back into her good graces. So, the retaliation began firing up as I tried to ignore it all, letting her insults and mean-spirited efforts to win me back roll off my back like the many "freak" comments hurled at me on a daily basis by our peers. One classmate told me that Sarah was telling some of our classmates that Tonya and I were "dykes," and that I was "insane." She was also repeating Todd's recollection of our fooling around session, laughing at his characterization of me.

"She really went for it, he said, and said she performed like someone who was starved for affection like a kid dying for a hamburger."

I felt like I couldn't escape her presence even though she was supposedly gone from my life.

"For someone who describes me as obsessive, she sure is obsessing over me a lot," I remember thinking often, prompting me to anger.

And the mounting animosity would come to a head.

Towards the sunset of April, mere days after the Columbine massacre, Tonya and I went on a class field trip to Old Sturbridge Village, a "living museum" in Massachusetts devoted to re-creating the atmosphere of early rural New England. At age 16, I found most of this old stuff pretty boring, but there were a couple of highlights. As I peered at a collection of ancient firearms behind a pane of glass, I noticed a sudden attraction to guns that I'd never felt before. I immediately connected the feeling to the Columbine massacre. In the past, news stories and fiction about shootings had always struck me as unoriginal. That was why I dug slasher movies and thought up odd ways for the kids to die in my Elks Club book. I'd never held a gun and never before wanted to. But now I was fascinated as I kept picturing two boys my age dressed in long black coats taking revenge on their peers.

Tonya and I had a ball with the disposable camera I'd brought along. Thanks to snapshots of us hamming it up in the bathroom and posing with museum staff in milkmaid costumes, I know exactly what I was wearing that day: a shimmery teal halter top and baggy jeans with a little rainbow stitch-work on one side. About a dozen black rubber bangles adorned my left arm, along with a black spiked bracelet and a furry leopard print bracelet with rhinestones. On my right, I sported thick rubber bangles in a rainbow of colors, filled with a sparkly liquid. After the break with Sarah, I'd decided to dress in a way that reflected my divided self: Elka, my dark alter ego, on the left and sunny Gina on the right.

The drive back to Vermont was punctuated with a stop at a mall where we got forty-five minutes to wander around our own. Tonya and I found a store called Hot Topic, where I paid a couple of dollars for a metal ring with a black and white circle around the word "Psycho" in a drippy font: a nod to the Hitchcock film. I stuck it on my right index finger. As we resumed our bus trip back to school, Tonya lent me her *Matrix* soundtrack CD. I popped it into my Discman and remembered watching a news program that blamed Columbine on violent movies. They'd shown a clip from *The Matrix*, featuring Keanu Reeves shooting people in slow motion, his trench coat whooshing up around him as bullets floated past. In front of me, a girl turned around and said something.

"Huh?" I pulled the headphones off my left ear, but I could still hear the music and feel the vibration.

"You two are a couple, right?" She meant Tonya and me.

"Uh—"

"You're hesitating, so that means yes." She smiled and batted her lashes.

"No, we are not," Tonya said. "We are best friends."

I was delighted to hear it: confirmation that my best friend crush was requited.

"That's not what I heard. I heard you two were lesbos." As she turned away, her vinyl seat cover squeaked, making a farting sound.

"Bitch," I whispered, rolling my eyes.

"Sarah's behind this, as per usual," Tonya concluded. I knew she was likely right.   Sarah seemed to repeat her homophobic storyline to anyone who would listen, unbothered by the way it contradicted her other favorite tale: that I was banging every guy I could get my hands on.

Tonya's car was in the shop that day, so we waited on the front steps at Spaulding until her mother could pick us up. Sarah's tan Honda was smack in our line of vision. It was what the legal profession would call an "attractive nuisance."

I watched Tonya squinting in that direction.

"Wish we had shaving cream," I said under my breath.

Tonya unzipped her black pleather backpack. She took out a notebook and pen.

"What are you doing?"

"You'll see," she smirked. Then, the sounds of excited scribbling. There were still nearly a dozen kids sitting on the steps. Most of them were probably waiting for rides.

She showed me the page. "You are a fucking fat ass bitch. Love, Stu," it said. The writing was big and sloppy, each word overlapping multiple thin blue lines.

I laughed and asked,"What are you doing with that?"

"Putting it on her windshield."

"You can't write that, she'll know it's us. Stu? She read the Elks book so many times!"

"Okay." And Tonya tried again.

"You fucking fatass whore. I'm gonna fucking kill you. Love, the Trench Coat Mafia." I looked at it and shrugged.

Yes, this was the moment that changed so many things in my life, and I let it happen with a shrug—without a moment's reflection.

"Well, I guess she won't be able to tell we wrote it." I laughed. The signature surprised me, since Tonya and I hadn't really talked over our reactions to the Columbine shooting. We acknowledged the event, but we didn't express any sympathy for the killers. Perhaps it was an unspoken bond based on our common status as social pariahs.

108

Tonya got up and walked down to Sarah's car, folding the note on the way. When I saw her slip it under a windshield wiper, my heart speeded up. I thought it was funny, but I also felt nervous. What if we got caught? This adrenaline mixed with gratitude: I was touched that she wanted to defend me, defend us, that I now had a best friend who would protect instead of insult me.

A few minutes later, Tonya's mom arrived. She was playing an AM station and I heard the news announcer talking about a rash of arrests across the country. Teens were getting in trouble for "copycat Columbine style plans."

Fuck, I thought, my heart pounding harder. Then I reassured myself: those were *real* threats backed up by actual plans. Our note was a simple joke.

Except it wasn't so simple. There was anger behind it. We were furious with Sarah, but we didn't want her dead. We just wanted to never see or hear from her again. That being impossible, I for one would have settled for a permanent end to her harassment. It wasn't crucial to me that the message include a death threat; the blast of generic meanness in the first note would have worked. But after everything she'd done to me, I wasn't stopping a death threat, either. That was my mindset. I didn't consider the presence of witnesses, and I didn't think she'd identify us as the note's authors. I thought she'd be briefly scared and forget about it. I was wrong.

My journal from that day reflects my casual attitude: "Today me and Tonya wrote a death threat and put it on Sarah's car. We wrote it from the Trench Coat Mafia. Ha ha. Actually, Tonya wrote it but it was funny. Got good shopping today, more halter tops and bindis, and a psycho ring."

From this point on, my journal entries fluctuate in the degree to which I considered myself responsible for the death threat. I would bounce back and forth, sometimes giving Tonya sole credit while portraying myself as a mere bystander. At other times I gave us equal credit, knowing that I influenced her scribbling. Sometimes, impressed by the note's outsized impact and the powerful feeling it gave me, I wished that I had been the one to write it. At times, I wished it were me so I could have shielded her from any responsibility; I felt guilty for involvement altogether. Other times, I regretted that it was written at all.

The next day, Tonya and I approached the school parking lot to find a cop pacing around her dusty red car. Circling, he looked like a shark in uniform.

"Oh no," we said, almost in unison, but didn't stop walking. He looked up at us. I could tell he was checking out my outfit: fishnets and a knee-length skirt with a dragon pattern on it.

He said he wanted to speak to us separately. He pointed to Tonya first. I sat in her car with the windows rolled up while he talked to her in another part of the lot. I could see some of our classmates standing in the lot and staring, taking an interest. Heart pounding, I looked down at my ring watch. I turned my "psycho" ring around so that the writing faced inward. Time was slowing down. I fiddled with the sun visor, moving it around and opening the mirror to look at myself. I wiped globs of eye liner out of my tear ducts. I kicked a plastic Mountain Dew bottle on the dirty, furry floor.

The passenger side door opened. I thought I might pass out. "Okay, your turn," the officer said.

Tonya opened the door on the driver's side and plopped into her seat. She shot me an exhausted look and rested her head back. Her straight, raven hair fell in front of her face.

"Your friend already confessed," said the cop as we stood in back of the car.

"She did?" I was shocked. It wasn't what I expected, but why would a cop lie?

"You're not planning to do another Columbine, are you?"

I stared into his Ron Swanson-esque mustache. It was thick, with hundreds of little black and brown hairs. The world felt shaky, like my voice. "No! God, no. We don't—we're not like that. We, well, we—"

I looked at a red pickup in a corner of the lot. A rifle hung on a rifle rack, framed by a ring of rust. I'd never noticed the gun before. I'd only paid attention to the truck because of its worn Sublime bumper sticker—a band I heard Evan liked.

"Why did you two write this?"

He held up a photocopy of the note. It looked different in black and white, the reproduction appearing flatter, distorted. The words "kill" and "Trench Coat Mafia" seemed to take on a more sinister cast.

"There are multiple witnesses who saw what you girls did."

My heart was going a mile a minute.

"We're also testing the note for fingerprints."

I shrugged. I couldn't imagine what to say.

"Why would you girls write such a vicious thing? You know this is something you could go to juvie for, if we find out you lied."

"This girl, well that girl, the one who got the note, she's been harassing us. We just wanted to scare her, I guess. We were just sick of it."

"So you aren't going to hurt anybody?"

"No!" I assured him. "Never!"

Before he left, he thanked me for my time. He said there would be an investigation. It was possible we'd be sent to juvenile detention for a few months. He'd be in touch.

"Are you going to call my parents?" That seemed like the worst thing. When he said yes, I thought: my mom is *actually* going to kill me.

I got into the car. Tonya drove. It took a while for either of us to speak.

"I can't believe that happened. Stupid Sarah," she began. "I didn't tell him anything," she added.

Oh no. "But he told me you confessed."

"WHAT? He lied. Did you—?"

"Yeah," I said. I hunkered down in my seat and looked away, out the window.

"Fuck!" she mashed on the gas pedal, hard. We rode in silence till she dropped me off in my driveway. I don't think we even said goodbye.

That next day I wrote a long journal entry that I think is worth quoting for what it reveals about my emotional reactions at the time. While barely noting the legal risk I'd run, I was devastated at the sense of having disgraced myself in Tonya's eyes and those of the school at large. Later in the day, as I started to bounce back, I expressed my satisfaction with the power we'd leveraged by threatening Sarah, as well as my forebodings as to how she'd retaliate.

04/30/99

I hate today! Sarah called the police about the note. Everyone in school knows, and in the parking lot the police officer was waiting for us. He talked with us separately. I should have denied it, but I thought Tonya already told him, and he played mind games. Plus he said they were gonna do fingerprints and said there were witnesses. I confessed that Tonya wrote the note. I should've said "I'm not admitting anything" but I thought Tonya had already confessed. Now Tonya hates me and the cops called my mom and told them so she called Tonya's mom. Tonya had told her mom that the cops were harassing *us* but claimed that we didn't do anything. Now my mom called them (Tonya's parents). I don't know what to do. I didn't want to lie to the police shithead because it wasn't a big deal, and if I lied it would be taken to court and I'd have a record. I dunno what to do now. The whole school knows. I knew I'd give into the manipulative officer. And, Tonya is mad because I didn't lie. I feel like a snitch, but I already thought she confessed. I hate myself. I'm an idiot.

Later in day:
Well, Tonya is no longer mad at me so I'm happy. She came over after her parents brought her to the police station. This incident, due to me and Tonya, was on radio and around school all day. And everyone was calling the police saying they should arrest us. They almost did. Sarah and her family tried to press charges on me, but the state court or whatever said no, it's not necessary. Thank God, because I could've spent up to a year in jail. It's funny how much impact I can make. I just know I'm gonna get a lot of shit at school on Monday, especially if it's in the paper tomorrow, which it'll probably be. I feel like Eric Harris on a very, very minor level. I can't believe Sarah was going to press charges. [...]I don't care if someone threatens to kill me. Big fucking deal. The note said, You fucking fatass whore. I'm gonna fucking kill you.

Love, the Trenchcoat Mafia. At least there was "love." Sarah is going to tell everyone.

And, for context, I myself had been the recipient of several death threats by this point. Some were suggestive, and anonymous, messages through AOL telling me I should "end" my "misery." Others were "funny" and also full of "love," hang up calls of "I love you and I'm going to kill you."

Though I barely mentioned my mother's role in all of this, I'd been pleasantly shocked when she didn't scream or scold me following the note. "I understand why you'd do something like that," she'd said as we sat in the kitchen. The afternoon sun was shining on her makeup-free face and the new blond highlights in her short, curly bob.

"What?" I was taken aback. Was Mom on my side?

"I know you didn't mean it."

She seemed relieved to know for sure that my relationship with Sarah was over and done with.

Reports of the Columbine killers being being bullied, and targeting the jocks who bullied them, began emerging within hours of the shooting and they were celebrated for it. Shooter Dylan Klebold's mom wrote in her memoir that her son and Eric were "heralded as champions for a cause.[12]" She said she received "chilling letters from alienated kids expressing admiration for Dylan and what he'd done. Adults who had been bullied as children wrote to tell us they could relate to the boys and their actions." Additionally, young men left messages on her answering machine calling Dylan a God and a hero. When footage from a video class project Eric and Dylan made leaked, showing the boys in trench coats, yelling at the camera, it "had become a rallying cry for bullied kids." Bullied kids, like myself, related to the murderers.

But, bullying wasn't the catalyst for the crimes, according to David Cullen, author of The New York Times best-selling true crime book Columbine. He claimed the two killers didn't care about targeting people who bullied them during their killing spree. Instead, they wanted to become more famous than the Timothy McVeigh, the man behind the Oklahoma City Bombing. Cullen showed that Eric was a sociopath who manipulated depressive, suicidal Dylan to help him with his sadistic plan to kill as many people as possible, and go down in history for it. Originally, he wanted to blow up Denver, but after he realized he was incapable of such a feat, he set his sights on their school. In an op-ed, Cullen wrote, "In a perfect world, Eric would extinguish the species. Eric was a practical kid, though. The planet was beyond him; even a block of Denver high-rises was out of reach. But he could pull off a high school.[13]"

Their body count was a blip in comparison to the destruction they had intended.

I didn't know any of this yet. I thought the boys merely snapped under the pressure of constant, everyday harassment as that was how I absorbed the media presentation of the tragedy. I fantasized about fighting back against bullies all the time. Would I ever think to actually kill anyone? No. But at this moment I assumed that I, too, could stand up to my harassers. But it turns out, I only shared sympathy with what the media said happened, not with the real killers.

"They weren't trying to punish the jocks," stated Cullen in a video about his book. "They were trying to terrorize the entire country on television, and if we are going to prevent more of these attacks, we have to start by understanding what happened here and why they did it.[14]"

This doesn't mean that they were never bullied in their high school career, or that some school shooters aren't badly bullied. However, bullying doesn't seem to be the motivating factor behind most school shooters' actions. In fact, Dr. Peter Langman profiled 48 of them in School Shooters: Understanding High School, College and Adult Perpetrators. Only one of the people profiled specifically targeted a bully.

The myth of the bullied school shooter isn't just incorrect. It is dangerous on several levels. It allows others to eye any kid who seems bullied with suspicion, and more often than not, it's the kid who doesn't fit in, the weird kid.

Like I was.

According to a study by Dr. Langman, school shooters are actually more likely to be bullies themselves than to be true victims of bullies. "Approximately 54% of the perpetrators [the 48 school shooters he studied] harassed, intimidated, threatened, or assaulted people prior to their attacks," he wrote[15]. He divided school shooters into three categories: psychopathic, psychotic, and traumatized. According to Langman, 94% of the psychopathic shooters, like Eric, bullied others. Only 18% of the psychopathic shooters were bullied, but 75% of the traumatized ones were. 60% of the shooters in Langman's study weren't bullied at all, and only one of the shooters specifically targeted a bully during their rampage.

CHAPTER 12

CAN YOU TELL ME IF YOU WANT TO KILL ANYONE?

Tonya and I lucked out when no charges were filed, but I knew that wouldn't be the end of it. The night after confessing in the parking lot, I dreamed that Sarah asked our English teacher if she could switch desks to sit further away from me. The very next day, that beautiful dream came true. Sarah made the request and the teacher complied. Was she truly scared or just putting on an act? I suspected it was the latter, but couldn't be sure. It was delicious to imagine that my ex-friend might be genuinely frightened of me. I wanted her to feel even a fraction of the pain she'd been putting me through. On the other hand, the actions she took next made me worry that she hadn't learned a thing, that she was out for revenge and would say anything to get it. If that was true, maybe Tonya and I had walked into a trap.

I got my first glimpse of what was coming out on the football field. My gym class was supposed to be practicing archery, but Tonya and I were goofing around, pretending our bows were swords and fencing with them. We chatted about our plans for prom weekend.

As we took turns shooting arrows, a sophomore girl approached. She was someone who'd never spoken to us before. She asked if we were going to prom.

I nodded.

"Who with?"

"No one, really. We're going together. As friends," Tonya said.

"Oh. I heard...some stuff." The girl was looking down, clutching her left upper arm with the opposite hand.

"Like what?" I assumed more tales about us being lesbians.

"Well, I heard a weird rumor that you two are planning on doing something crazy at prom."

"Like what?" Tonya asked.

"Like, a shooting spree kind of thing."

Tonya and I locked eyes. I gaped in shock. Then I had to laugh.

"I mean, you guys do look the type. At least you do, Gina. No offense."

"What?! I don't even have a gun!" The loud volume of my response surprised me.

"It's just what I heard. Thought I'd check." The sophomore shrugged. "They said something about a prom book or something. So, you don't have plans to do anything?"

"Of course not! Are you kidding?!"

She turned and began walking to the other edge of the field, where most of our classmates were. I waited until I was sure she was out of earshot to ask Tonya, "Is this about the note?"

"But she said a book. No note."

"Do you think she means the Elks Club book?" The world around me suddenly looked too sunny, so bright it was almost white.

"Maybe. How would she know about it, though?"

"Sarah. Oh, my God, it's her."

We tried to convince ourselves that it might just be a minor rumor. Maybe she'd only told a few people about this bizarre theory about prom. Maybe the story wouldn't spread very far. I kept running my pointer finger over the red and white bristles at the end of the bow. Kara, a popular girl, was sitting out of the activity. She was sitting on the bleachers, with her head down, real quiet and sullen. It seemed out of character. She was always peppy and chatty. Just the other week, she talked to me while we were playing kickball on the grassy field; because she was nice to me on that sunny April afternoon,   I beamed like a sun beam shining through a cloud.

After gym I had keyboard class, taught by a plump blonde in a baby pink sweater set. The classroom telephone rang. She answered it and said, "Okay, I'll tell her."

Sure it was for me, I slumped in my plastic seat.

"Gina, you need to go down to the office."

Soon I faced the vice principal.   Mrs. Minart was a short, dark-haired woman with a southern accent.

"Gina, it's nice to meet you."

Before her on her desk was the laminated photocopy of the death threat.

"I want to talk about this," she said, "As well as this Elks Club book I've been hearing about."

"I don't want to say anything unless my mom is here." After I'd confessed to that cop, my mom had told me never to talk to police or school officials without her or a lawyer in the room.

"Can you tell me if you want to kill anyone?"

"Of course I don't want to kill anyone. Now I don't want to say anything else."

Mrs. Minart agreed that my mom could come in, but it had to be soon.

What happened next was horrible for me and Tonya, but it could have been a lot worse. Other students who made non-serious threats or merely joked inappropriately in the aftermath of the Columbine massacre were actually arrested. Some of them went to jail. And the pattern that manifested after the shooting would be reinforced after later massacres.   In my capacity as a freelance journalist, I once interviewed a mother whose 16-year-old son had spent about a year in prison for verbal threats he made. The whole thing blew up "because of the small town hysteria, especially after the [Sandy Hook] shootings," she told me in 2013. "He wasn't going to be charged, but after Newtown, he got arrested. There were no weapons found and no hit list." In prison, he became anxious and depressed. He felt that he had ruined his life. Once out, he was on probation, kept on a tight watch. He got into trouble again for smoking weed.

The fact that Tonya and I were never locked up was largely a function of happenstance, a twist of fate I'll always be grateful for. Post 9/11, we might not have been so lucky.   Likely, we would have been charged with making terroristic threats.

Well before my mom came in to have the session with Mrs. Minart, things at Spaulding were spinning out of control. All it took was the sight of Tonya and me entering the cafeteria for the room to erupt in a chorus of contempt.

"The psychos are here!"

"That's them!"

Someone threw a half-eaten candy bar, which landed in front of us.

"Let's get the fuck out of here," Tonya said. We went to the library and sat at a table not far from Nadine, my former friend from junior high. Nadine was the one who had slow danced with Evan. The two of us hadn't spoken since seventh grade. She glared at me and loudly huffed, packed her stuff, and left in a hurry. I realized she must have been informed that I'd killed her off in my Elks Club book. I felt humiliated.

When I signed onto AOL that night, I was instantly bombarded. Every time I closed one message box, a new one popped up. Many were from classmates I'd never talked to in person.

Ding

"Do you really wanna kill everybody?"

Ding

"Fuck you, psycho."

Ding

"Why do you want to murder my friend?"

Ding

"I heard you want to kill my sister."

I wrote back to the last one, because I was growing increasingly interested in who was on my supposed hit list. I said, "I don't want to kill anyone. Who's your sister?"

She told me. I didn't even know her sibling.

It wasn't all bad; there were supportive messages, too. Though some supporters chose to stay anonymous, others were open, and it surprised me when a few popular students reached out to me. Some people seemed to be trying to distance themselves from their friends' bullying. Maybe they just didn't want to get shot in the event that the rumors were true.

The rumors were endless, but most fell into two groups: those about me wanting to shoot up or blow up the school that Friday and those about me wanting to shoot up or blow up the prom on Saturday. There were colorful details like the story about my plan to plant a bomb in the cafeteria's popcorn machine.

I called Tonya and heard that she'd only received one message. Apparently the rumors mostly focused on me. People were saying that I had an accomplice, but didn't seem to know who that person was. It figured, I thought, since I stuck out on account of my clothing.

Soon the rumors touched my family. My brother's sixth grade classmates asked him why I wanted to kill their older siblings. One threatened to beat him up. A coworker of my dad's claimed to have heard from a "reliable source" that I'd stocked up on weapons. Our minister called my mom to see how she was holding up. Some of her colleagues believed I was guilty of plotting to blow up the school.

I was stunned by the sheer variety of the rumors. In addition to the bomb in the popcorn machine, there was the one about how Tonya and I had placed a white cross on the front lawn at Spaulding, then draped it with a black trench coat. Another one, based on my Elks Club book and its mocking of Glofs, was that I planned to kill anyone whose name began with the letters L, M, or N. I overheard people saying that I'd drafted lists of proposed victims conforming to that pattern. True, this contradicted other rumors identifying supposed targets whose names all began with other letters. But the fact that my story seemed to be having a real world effect—that my imagination had such power to terrify—was undeniably exciting.

The closer it got to prom that week the more the rumors escalated. Tonya and I tried to stay away from the cafeteria and halls. We hid out in the library and dissected the online chatter.

"One person said I wanted to kill Jen LeClair. Why her?" I wondered.

"Because Sarah hates her, remember?" Tonya ran long fingers through the white streaks in her hair. "And I guess she hooked up with Evan, too. It fits the you-wanna-murder-Evan thing." She winked, then added, "Which we all know is partially true."

I smiled. I always felt bashful when anyone touched on my obsession for Evan. Even though she'd said kill, it felt much the same. But then I thought that he probably hated me now because of the murder rumors.

Truthfully, I said I hadn't known about the hookup. "I don't fucking care. I have nothing against Jen. As far as I know, she never made fun of me."

After lunch period, Tonya had a science class. I headed upstairs to English. As I walked the length of the hall, classmates stared at me. They were quiet at first, then loud. Very loud.

"Psycho!" someone yelled. I'd been called that before, but this was the moment when the word on my ring crystallized into a new identity. From this point on, I would learn to answer to it as readily as if somebody called me "Gina."

A bunch of boys in hunting gear jostled past. One pushed me in the shoulder. "Hey killer," he said loudly.

As I neared my locker, I could hear the muttering. "That's the girl that wants to kill everyone."

"She really does. I heard it from her old best friend," came a voice from the staring crowd.

"I mean, she *looks* like a psycho!"

I opened my locker. Evan walked towards me. His eyes were cold and distant. I noticed the frosted tips on his once dark hair. Was this a recent thing? It seemed like if I really cared about him, I should have noticed the change in his hair. As he passed, he mumbled something. It sounded unfriendly. It hit me then that he may likely believe that I actually wanted to murder him.

It felt as though I had just been shot in the back of the head and the gut simultaneously with all my embarrassing secrets, embellished with even more embarrassing lies, bleeding out of me onto the hallway for everyone to see.

I wanted to cry, but I kept my expression stoic. People were yelling, pointing, throwing pieces of crumpled paper. Three kids ran past holding books above their heads, giggling as they called, "Duck and cover!"

And at the other end of the hallway stood Sarah, surrounded by classmates wearing fleece and Abercrombie and Fitch. She was laughing. No, cackling.

It felt like this was all just a sick joke to everyone, an amped-up version of familiar mockery. I questioned whether anyone was genuinely frightened.

I soon learned that some people were. Back at my locker a few hours later, Tonya told me that Kara, whose name appeared on my rumored kill list, wanted to drop out of gym because of me. "People were reading that list in my math class," she reported, adding that people spoke of my supposed "accomplice" but apparently didn't realize she was sitting right there. "I guess she also hooked up with Evan. That's what Ben said, anyway."

"Oh my *God*," I began loudly, then remembered to lower my voice. "What a nightmare. This is fucking embarrassing. The kill-people-who-dated-Evan list!"

I thought of how sullenly she was sitting in gym class on the bleachers. This was why.

"I hear there's gonna be a massacre this week," a guy said, walking past us.

"It's really more for your protection than anybody else's," Mrs. Minart said. It was Thursday. Sitting next to Mom, I nodded and fingered the tape recorder I'd snuck into a pocket of my baggy denim pants. I kept checking to make sure both the "play" and "record" buttons were pressed down.

"Parents have apparently made some threats against Gina's life if she shows up at the Elks Club," Mrs. Minart went on.

"Yes, we know." Mom sounded impatient already.

I remembered the adrenaline rush of hearing kids saying that their parents planned to stake out the Elks Club parking lot, armed with shotguns and on alert. Earlier that day, a Channel 3 news van had showed up in front of school; I'd watched as a reporter interviewed a classmate. I couldn't believe the impact I'd had by writing —well, helping write—a few words. Or was it the words I wrote in the Elks Club book that were causing this? It was all so confusing.

It all totally sucked, so why did it feel kind of good?

Mrs. Minart asked if I was sure that I didn't want to hurt anyone.

"Yes, of course I'm sure."

"Have you ever even imagined hurting anyone else?"

My mom closed her eyes. I knew why she was preemptively mad. She wanted me to be careful, but I *hated* lying. For some reason I thought that full disclosure would be in my best interests.

"Well, yes. I've imagined hurting others." Mom sighed and darted her eyes at me, as if to say she thought I carried honesty too far. "But never *killing* them!" I elaborated. "Have I imagined punching people who bully me? Sure, but not that often."

Mrs. Minart frowned. Perhaps she shared my mother's view of my honesty.

"The only person I've actually hurt or ever would hurt is myself." Mom's look was telling me to stop.

"What do you mean?"

"Like, I have cut myself at times. Just to deal with things, not trying to kill myself."

"But you'd never do that to anyone else."

I shook my head: no.

Mrs. Minart wondered if my account of the bullying was exaggerated. "I followed you and Tonya to lunch the other day, and I didn't see anyone harassing you."

I protested that the one time we'd been to the cafeteria, the reaction was so crazy that we had to leave. "That was the only time we went to lunch all week. The rest of the days, we've been in the library. What day did you follow us?"

She responded by changing the subject. "What about this kill list people are talking about?"

I denied making a kill list. I didn't know the rumors' source. "I think Sarah made it all up."

"Could it be something from your prom book?"

"It's not a 'prom book.' It just takes place at the Elks Club."

"The prom takes place at the Elks Club."

"That book is about a *sixth grade dance.*" It was finally hitting me what bad luck I was cursed with, having my junior prom scheduled for that particular venue. But then again, there weren't a lot of venues in the area to begin with.

"Look, this is very hard for me." Mrs. Minart turned to my mom. "I've never seen these girls before. None of them. I'm not used to disciplining honor students."

Mom nodded, one educator to another. Mrs. Minart turned back to me.

"We—I mean myself, the principal, and our school therapist—want to take a look at your prom book."

"I already told you, it's not a prom book. It has nothing to do with this prom."

"Okay, then you won't mind us seeing it."

I looked at Mom and back to Mrs. Minart. I was confused why she was focusing so much on this story rather than the actual threat.

"You'll probably just find something wrong with it anyway. I'm scared you'll see something threatening when it's not there." My sudden boldness shocked me. I never even spoke in class, not unless I couldn't get out of it. My good grades all came from my written work.

Mrs. Minart went on explaining her conditions. If I handed over the Elks Club book, I'd get one day of out of school suspension (Friday), plus two days of in school suspension on Monday and Tuesday. It meant that I couldn't go to prom, but my record would stay clean. If I chose to withhold the book, I'd get three days out of school and it would go on my record.

"The book's not threatening, just weird," I insisted. "There's a dancing triangle in it, and a monkey, too. Right, mom? You read it." The minute I said that, I remembered her reaction. She'd called it "disturbing." Would she back me up now?

To my great surprise, she not only affirmed that the story wasn't threatening, she said she'd called the school multiple times in the past to complain I was being bullied. "Nothing was ever done. I specifically complained to Gina's math teacher about Sarah's behavior. Now the principal is refusing to talk to us, but making statements to the news crews outside. If *this* doesn't warrant talking to a student's parents, what the hell does?"

This was stunning. I'd had no idea. Yes, I knew she'd complained about educational content, like the "dumbed-down" version of *Great Expectations*. But I never dreamed she'd called about me being bullied. It was something I hoped I'd successfully hidden from her. Now I was embarrassed just as much as I was grateful.

Mrs. Minart said she'd talked with some of my teachers and nobody brought up my being targeted by peers. Her response, I know now, was typical of the way a lot of schools approached this issue in a decade when bullying tended not to be taken seriously. Teachers protected themselves by claiming ignorance; administrators were even less courageous.

Mom sternly told Mrs. Minart that the two of us would discuss the Elks Club story with "our lawyer."

As we headed to her car, she told me a story about running into a neighbor, Sammy's mom, on the way to the appointment. Sammy was my brother's good friend, and our families always spent the Fourth of July together, eating barbecue and setting off firecrackers. "She said to me, 'I guess sometimes our kids aren't as perfect as we think they are.' She didn't even ask if the rumors were true. She didn't ask to help. Fuck her."

"Mom!" I was shocked. "I never hear you swear like that."

"You're my daughter and I'm here to protect you."

It was one of the most comforting things she ever said to me. When it came to offering consolation she and Dad were pretty hopeless; I never felt like I could confide in them. But looking back, I know how much she loved me. She fought for me. Her actions spoke for her.

As six o'clock approached, Tonya and I sat in my family's den waiting for the Channel 3 news to come on. At 5:55, they ran a promo for the broadcast. "Rumors rattle Spaulding High," the announcer proclaimed. A picture of our school flashed on the screen.

"Aw shit, we should press record now!" I started the VCR.

"I bet we're top of the news," Tonya said.

She was right.

"Echoes of school shootings past are resounding loud and clear in Barre," the news anchor stated with a serious look. "The junior prom — a night for young fun — will have police patrols this Saturday. Rumors of a threat — a shooting threat —have officials on edge."

He emphasized that a reporter on the scene had "more on what's put a dark cloud of danger over prom night."

That phrase,

dark cloud of danger

immediately clung to my brain.

The story featured footage from a recent shooting at a graduation dance in Pennsylvania—teens in formal dresses, crying; an interview with one of Evan's best friends from middle school wearing a varsity jacket, who said that the local rumors of "a girl shooting people" on top of the carnage in Littleton were making people nervous; and our principal, Bill Sullivan, who reassured the public that every tip and rumor had been investigated, ensuring that "the prom on Saturday will be safer than it was a year ago." A reporter reinforced this message. Speaking over a tight shot of the Elks Club sign, followed by a wide shot of the brick edifice with its lawn, flagpole, and American flag, she indicated that the prom's location might be changed at the last minute. "There will be extra faculty and several police officers on patrol. Spaulding's principal says it's necessary in the brave new world of school violence—one that heightens fears and allows rumors to spin out of control."

It was so surreal that I felt high. For a moment there, I got the sensation of being *inside* the Columbine coverage I'd watched just a few days before. I wished the segment had lasted even longer.

"Wow," Tonya said. "Fucked up."

"We made the news! It may not be for something good, but— "

"We did something, all right." She laughed.

I was definitely enjoying the attention. At the same time, I was annoyed that the reporter had gotten some of her facts wrong. She'd called my book a "five-year-old work of fiction" concerning a "tragedy at a prom."

"And that cut from the Elks Club to Columbine, jeez! It looks like people are running out of the Elks!"

The high wore off. Later that night, while listening to my Discman, I got so angry that I ripped my headphones off and threw the device against my dresser. It still worked, but part of it was dented. Tonya, I later learned, had reacted physically too, punching a hole in the wall of her family's computer room.

The next day, a school acquaintance let me know that she'd gone to Mrs. Minart along with Tonya's and my friend Krystal to tell her what they'd witnessed: Sarah actively spreading rumors and distributing a "kill list" that she attributed to me. Mrs. Minart, I learned, had told the two of them that I'd admitted cutting myself. This "disturbed" her, she claimed.

"That was supposed to be confidential," I said. Talk about disturbing!

I was still resisting handing over the Elks Club book.

My parents hired a lawyer, who, after making a few calls to the school and local news outlets, thought it would be best if I handed over the manuscript. This I did, reluctantly. The school therapist then reviewed it and decided that it definitely wasn't a prom-killing manual—nor a school shooting story in any shape or form. However, he did say that it was very disturbing—that word again—and I needed to get immediate therapy. The school went forward with the promised punishment: three days' suspension off the record for Tonya and me. We couldn't be in school on Friday, the day of our rumored school shooting plan, and on prom night, Saturday, we had to stay home under adult supervision.

I couldn't stop rewinding and re-watching the Channel 3 story. Even though it wasn't completely accurate, it gave me a rush. Look at what I did. Even though I didn't exactly *do* anything.

Except it kind of felt that way. Wasn't this uproar because of me?

Us. Because of us.

I remembered joking, "We did something, all right." It felt like a form of power.

CHAPTER 13

INFAMY

Tell Saddam
not to bother making a bomb
because Gina Tron
is gonna crush the prom

When I woke up, this song was stuck in my head. I lay there, replaying the moment when two Spaulding boys had sung it at me. My digital alarm clock said 8:55. It was Friday, May 7, the first morning of Tonya's and my three-day off-the-record suspension. On Monday and Tuesday, we'd have in-school suspension, but today we were required to stay home. School officials wanted to ensure our absence from the scene on the date when our rumored plot to shoot up the school was supposed to be implemented.

I didn't want to get up. I remained horizontal and scanned my crowded walls. There were so many posters and magazine clippings of Courtney Love and Marilyn Manson and anonymous models in thick black eyeliner that there was little bare wall space left. Next to my bed I'd hung a graphic of the word "hate," spelled out with objects. A chrome-plated handgun served as the lower case "h."

I heard the landline start to ring downstairs; a slight delay and my own phone lit up. Groggily, I answered.

"Fuck you," said a young male voice. Then the dial tone.

Another one. I crawled back under the covers.

The phone rang again. I picked up, but this time didn't offer a greeting.

"Gina?" It was Tonya. She suggested driving over. "May as well hang together," she said.

Feeling a weird mix of dread and excitement, I showered and dressed. My mind dwelt on the remarkable fact that everyone in town was thinking about me, but all the same, I knew that nothing had changed. Nobody cared to hear my side of the story. At Spaulding, doors were locked and police were there; the atmosphere must be tense. I figured some kids had stayed home—all because of that note, or was it the Elks Club book?

Tonya arrived. "There are eggs on your house."

"Yeah, I know."

"When did that happen?"

"Day before yesterday." I thought of the mess on the side of our house that faced the dirt road. Little pieces of white shell were stuck in dried yellow ooze. "There's just so *much* going on. It's overwhelming."

"Totally. I get it." Tonya plopped into a kitchen chair, her shoulders hunched. Tall as she was, she looked a bit vulture-like.

"This is so fucking stupid. We've never even shot any guns," I said. "We're probably just about the only people in school who don't have guns in our houses. But Sarah has plenty, thanks to her racist dad!"

Tonya corrected me. "My brother has guns under his bed."

"Oh." It made sense. He'd recently joined the military.

"Rifles, my grandfather's old ones."

"Do they work?" I felt confused. Did she want us to use them? Or was I starting to get as paranoid as all the rumor-mongers?

She said she didn't think they were usable.

"Well, a lot of our classmates bring their hunting rifles to school." I was agitated, talking fast. "Like, not *into* school, but they leave them in the parking lot." I remembered the rifle racked in that old pickup with the Sublime sticker, the one I'd stared at while the policeman questioned me.

"Aren't they more likely than us to do something like Columbine?" I went on. "And what about Kyle Benoit? He's been building pipe bombs since fifth grade."

Tonya nodded. I looked out the kitchen window to the open expanse of land that filled up with tall grass in summer, and in winter hosted a snowmobile trail. Once while I was eating a bowl of cereal, I'd looked through that window and spotted our twelve-year-old neighbor, a kid with developmental problems and violent tendencies, pointing a rifle at the sky. That had given me a jolt. I wanted to feel some electricity on my prom night, too, even if it was uncomfortable. Under any circumstances, there was an aura to prom, a legendary quality that all the crazy rumors had only intensified. It felt like there had to be a climax, and I craved the chance to experience that, or at least witness it.

"I think we should still go out," I said. "Before prom, in our dresses. I really want to wear my damn dress." I'd been looking forward to that moment for so long, saving up my allowance for months to pay for the garment. Long and tight, made of baby blue velvet, it had a low-cut top with tiny straps. The skirt draped at the bottom.

Tonya agreed. We could go out to dinner before our curfew started.

"Yeah!" I could see the possibilities. "If any of our supposedly scared classmates spot us, maybe they'll think we're going to prom after all, and they'll spread that shit around."

We laughed, cheered by the realization that being excluded from the main event didn't mean we couldn't have an impact.

Still giddy from our role in last night's local news broadcast, we couldn't wait to see how the newspaper would cover all the craziness we'd help set in motion. I hoped we'd be prominently featured, maybe with a focus on my Elks Club story. The minute I saw the paper delivery jeep speeding up our road, churning up dirt like tiny tornadoes, I turned to Tonya. "Let's take a walk."

As we stepped outside, I asked, "You got the chocolate?" That was code for cigarettes, our only real vice. We smoked socially, mostly in each other's company. Tonya nodded and pulled a pack of Marlboro Lights out of her purse. Using my silver Cheshire cat Zippo lighter, I lit one and inhaled, enjoying the immediate rush to my head even if the smoke made my teeth feel nasty. I passed the lighter to Tonya.

Having climbed the steep driveway, we came to the road. As we crossed, a snake slithered between us: gray, with a red belly.

"Oooh, snakey," Tonya squealed.

"Yeah, I used to catch those guys when I was a kid."

Reaching our mailbox, I yanked the paper out and took a look. "First page, baby," I exulted—and not only that, it was the very top item. The headline read, "All Is Calm At Spaulding" over a sub-head: "304 Students Stay Out of School Today." The story emphasized the confidence of both police and school officials that rumors of plans to unleash violence in the school building or at the prom were completely unfounded. At the same time, it stressed all the measures being taken to "make sure everyone feels safe" and "demonstrate that we're taking this seriously," as Principal Sullivan put it. He was given space to debunk some of the more bizarre rumors, telling reporters that "there was no crucifix with a black trench coat planted in the lawn in front of the school, there was no bomb found in the popcorn machine and no evidence that the school's Bosnian students were plotting revenge for the NATO air assault on Yugoslavia." (The final item in the list referenced the fact that several Bosnian students who had recently come to Barre as refugees from the war in their native country were supposed to be joining up with me to spread mayhem.)

The most direct nods in Tonya's and my direction were lines about "the discovery of a threatening note on a student's car" and "the revelation of a short story allegedly authored by another student." The article closed with comments from our classmates. My first kiss' brother claimed to be genuinely frightened and thought school should have been canceled. Another suggested that some had deliberately spread wild stories in hopes of getting a day off.

I passed the paper to Tonya, who read as she smoked. We were now back on the lawn in front of my egg-besmirched house."We need to get scrapbooks to keep track of all this," she said.

"That's a great idea. Wonder if they have them at the mall?"

"We'll have to go and see. Well, maybe not now, but in a few days when all this madness calms down."

Next, I called Krystal. Because she still kept her connection with us while mostly hanging out with somewhat popular kids at Spaulding, she could provide information we couldn't get any other way. I wanted the inside dirt on what was going on at school.

She reported that things were strange; she'd only stayed for one period.

"Strange how?"

"Eerie. I mean, obviously some people were making a big joke of it. Some people were wearing football helmets in case of gunfire."

I laughed.

"Nothing eventful happened, at least while I was there. But, Gina—a lot of people and their parents—they want you expelled. They'll attack you if you show up at prom. At least that's the talk."

"I mean," I smirked, "can't believe *every* rumor, right?"

Despite—or maybe because of—Krystal's warning, I felt like showing up at the Elks Club, just to see. Again, I had that craving for a jolt of excitement. As Friday wore on, Tonya and I joked about dressing up, bringing suitcases to prom, suitcases plastered with stickers of guns. We'd fill them with candy. With all of the drama circling around us, touched off by our actions, it didn't make sense to stay on the sidelines.

We joked, but a part of me really wanted to do it.

"They are gonna try to push me over the edge so I kill, but I won't," I wrote in my journal that week.

Saturday came. Before dressing for a prom that I would not attend, I perused the day's newspaper. Another front page article revealed that on Friday, Spaulding had been "As Normal As It Could Be." Mostly a rehash of the previous day's coverage, it nevertheless included a few more details about the security measures planned for the Elks Club. There would be a police patrol, and someone at the door would check students for weapons. Later, I clipped the piece for my scrapbook. Next to it, I wrote my thoughts about Sarah: "All this bullshit happened to me and Tonya because of this psycho. It takes a real psychopath to take the time and effort out of their life into making someone else look psycho."

I put on my blue velvet dress, adding black fishnet arm bands and elastic around my middle fingers. Feeling loosed from all restraints, I applied even more black eyeliner than usual. My lashes were black and thick as if coated with tar. While I always made up my eyes, I'd noticed that when I styled them the way I liked best, smoky or with wings, people got on my case even more than usual. But now that there seemed to be so little relation between my behavior and people's reactions, I figured I might as well do as I pleased.

Mom walked into my room as I globbed black lipstick onto my lips. "You know, Gina, after this weekend you should probably tone things down. Just to keep a low profile."

"But that's like giving up, or giving in."

"It might make your life a little easier."

I wasn't convinced.

"You know I'm not one to hinder your self-expression. Right, Gina?"

I had to agree.

"So can you please, for me, once prom is over, just go without black makeup and dog collars. Especially no Marilyn Manson shirts. Just for a few weeks."

I sighed. I knew that Marilyn Manson concerts were being canceled, especially those scheduled anywhere near Colorado, out of respect for the Columbine victims. Tonya and I would later mock that decision, insisting that the lyrics to the widely adored pop hit "Livin' La Vida Loca" were far more disturbing than Manson's offerings. "It will make you go insane, like a bullet to your brain"— why was that respectable fare?

Reluctantly, I agreed to do as Mom said—"just for a little bit"—even though I couldn't see what good it would do. I said no when she renewed her proposal to transfer me to another school where I could start over. My loyalty to Tonya didn't waver, as I didn't want to leave her behind as I don't think she had the option to leave. I couldn't bear the thought of never seeing Evan again. In part, I didn't want to do anything that could be read as an admission of guilt, but there was more to it than that. The fact was, the whole thing felt almost good, like poking at a bruise.

Mom drove me to Tonya's. We didn't talk. I turned on the radio; "All Star" by SmashMouth was playing. It was probably the fourth or fifth time I heard the song, which was just starting to be played everywhere. A few lines spoke directly to me: "Well, the years start coming, and they don't stop coming. Fed to the rules, and I hit the ground running." I thought of all the years I was in love with Evan, all the years I spent trying to fit in. Then I pictured my classmates running, trying to dodge a rain of bullets. This is the fantasy that not only terrifies but secretly attracts them, I thought. Everyone needs a villain, and they made me one.

"Be safe," Mom said. Her green eyes squinted in sunlight that made them sparkle.

"I will."

"I love you."

"Love you too, Mom."

Tonya was in her kitchen, grabbing a soda from the fridge. She told me my dress looked awesome. She'd applied black lipstick, which made me happy—confirmation, I thought, that the two of us were united in our status as Spaulding's true oddballs. But she wasn't wearing any other makeup, and instead of her own prom dress, she had on a long black skirt and leopard print tank top. I guessed she hadn't been able to bring herself to put on the dress when we weren't even going.

My own disappointment was intense. I'd watched so many prom movies, and they all contributed to my vision of prom as a rite of passage. For years, I'd fantasized about a prom experience along the lines of *Pretty in Pink*. Now prom was here and I had to admit that on some level it did feel like I was in a movie, but not a very good one.

We got Tonya's mom to take our "prom" photos. Grinning, we posed with copies of the papers reporting on our ordeal. Then we were off for our prom dinner "date" at a cheap steak restaurant that was a fixture in Barre.

On the way there, Tonya told me that her aunt's family out in Michigan was going through more or less the same thing we were. Her cousin, a high school senior, had been suspended after calling in a bomb threat. It wasn't clear if he'd been serious or not.

"I guess it runs in the family," I quipped.

Tonya laughed and said the whole thing was surreal. "I just can't believe it's happening. I'm really sorry you're getting the worst of it."

I shrugged and said it wasn't her fault.

"I mean, it kinda is."

"Yeah, and it's my fault for writing the Elks Club book."

"Let's just blame Sarah."

"Yeah, if she was so fucking scared, like she told the police, why spread all those rumors?"

"And a fucking fake hit list."

We pulled into the restaurant's parking lot. Around us, classmates in long fluffy easter-egg-colored gowns were floating into the restaurant. I noticed their hems dragging on the pavement. My heart began beating hard. I wanted to tell Tonya to drive back to her house, but at the same time, I wanted to leap out of the car and give my richly adorned classmates the scare they deserved. The urge to chase them was strong, and new, and surprising. To retreat, or terrorize? Of course, we did neither. We went inside and sat down. Our faces stoic, we ordered steak. The waitress was rude to us, and at the neighboring tables we could hear some of our classmates loudly debating whether we'd be barred from prom.

"Margie said that if they show up at the Elks, they'll be arrested or even worse," said a girl with her auburn hair in an updo. Her yellow floral patterned dress reminded me of wallpaper: hideous, I thought. If everyone was going to judge what I wore, maybe it was time for me to judge them back.

I stared at the auburn-haired girl until her eyes met mine. Heart pounding, I winked at her. Her eyes got big and then she looked away. She shut her mouth and picked up a fork, which she held awkwardly.

I'd made someone cower. This was new, this recognition that I had power to do that to someone. It felt strange but kind of nice. I was so used to cowering myself, being on the receiving end of others' intimidation. My power lay in my notoriety. I didn't even know this girl's last name, yet I was on her mind—all because I was *infamous*.

When we got back from dinner we changed out of our fancy outfits, and later that night Tonya's mom took us to get ice cream, the supervised outing being permissible under the terms of our curfew. As we stood in line waiting for our treats, people driving by yelled "psycho" and "killer." We retreated to Tonya's and watched *Practical Magic*, about two witch sisters who lived in a close-minded small town. As relevant as the subject matter was to our own situation, I lost interest. Right now, real life was a lot more exciting than any movie. I felt like I'd rather re-watch the news story about us.

After the movie, Mom picked me up. At home in my bed, I lay wide awake. As I listened to rain and wind slam the house, I couldn't stop thinking about prom. Were there really armed parents staking out the parking lot? Were Tonya and I the number one conversation topic? I pictured the scene inside the Elks Club with all the dancing couples. I'd always hoped I'd get to slow dance with someone at prom. Which of my classmates were making out right now? Who was having sex? As thunder sounded in the distance, I cried myself to sleep.

Our in-school suspension began on Monday. Tonya and I did our time in a small room inside the administration building across the street from Spaulding. I could see the school every time I turned around to look through the tiny open window behind me. It was lovely out, the kind of spring day that feels so good it hurts. Tonya and I tried and failed to amuse ourselves. I'd brought along Stephen King's *Carrie* and one of my journals, while Tonya provided a tray of miniature pastries. The pastries were made to look like little pigs in blankets, but filled with strawberry-flavored goo instead of a hot dog. They didn't taste very good.

I was on my period, and after a few hours my pad needed changing. I dreaded talking to the middle-aged school employee who was acting as our guard, stationed on a chair outside our punishment room. I felt she hated me. But I could feel a wet dampness spreading between my legs. Shouldering my iridescent silver bag, I got up to ask permission.

In the doorway I paused, smiling awkwardly, trying to make eye contact. The woman wore a plain sweater and a silver necklace with a cross charm. Her lips were thin, chapped. She looked at me with dead, hawk-like eyes.

"Um, can I use the bathroom?"

"You *may.*"

"Where is it?" I wanted to disappear.

"To the left, first door." She sounded angry I'd asked.

I changed my pad in the tiny bathroom, so cramped I could touch the door while sitting on the toilet. I felt like I was in a confessional, but where were the adults who wanted to *really* listen to me? I remembered our minister calling to see how Mom was doing. What about me and my welfare? The cold of the seat on my legs provided relief from the unusual spring heat. As I returned to the punishment room, the hostile woman snapped at me, reminding me to leave the door open so she could see what we were doing.

I sat back down in front of a stupid painting, a red blob with legs that reminded me of the period blood I just saw, and paged through my copy of *Carrie,* a book I'd selected to signal my defiance. (This was before Stephen King disclosed that he both hated and pitied the title character, going so far as to compare her to the Columbine killers[16], a comment that left me feeling personally attacked.)

Next, I turned to my journal, the front cover of which was labeled "Day Dreams" and had an illustration of what looked like a Greek palace: pillars and a view of blue sky, green pastures, clumps of trees. The back cover showed a glassless window looking out on a night time scene with a fountain, a zebra, and a hedge maze that reminded me of *The Shining.* A shooting star streaked across the sky above the words "Night Dreams." I had intended to put entries about bad days in the dark side and good days in the sunny side, but soon realized that most of my days were a mix. "I'm in in-school suspension sitting in a room staring at a painting that I used to see at Barre Town Elementary School. At least I will be stronger in future or whatever. I knew something would happen involving the prom/Elks Club. It was inevitable. Sarah, I knew would do this to me one of these days."

I had turned the inside cover of *Night Dreams* into a mini memorial to Eric Harris and Dylan Klebold, Scotch taping newsprint reproductions of their grainy yearbook photos next to an "R.I.P" that meant more to me than ever. Once I was accused of being like them, I felt closer to them; I truly believed they'd been ostracized. And their infamy, their badass-itude, made them sexier than any boy band. On the "Day Dreams" side, I'd drawn a flower with an R.I.P. for a classmate who'd died. When she first entered Spaulding, she'd hung out with me in gym class and we even skipped it once together, but that only lasted for a few weeks. Later, she sat with the girls who threw French fries at me in the cafeteria.

At some point Evan's girlfriend, a tall, smoky-eyed blonde, came to drop something off with our receptionist-guard, who made a point of asking loudly, "How was prom?"

"It was good. It was safe. Very *safe*," the girlfriend said, her eyes shooting beams at me. She left, tossing her long blond beauty queen hair behind her. I wrote on the "Day Dreams" side of my journal: "Oh look, Evan's girlfriend just gave me a dirty look. I wonder why! He thought I was gonna kill him. Another goal? Maybe!" Even though I was angry and hurt, getting a reaction like that from such a popular girl—one who hadn't bothered to notice my existence up until now—did seem to confirm my importance. At the same time, I felt a stark sense of loss. A piece of me was gone. I knew that Evan, who meant so much to me, must now regard me with fear, disgust, or both. I was indignant to think he assumed I'd be a fan of his forever, even though I suspected that was probably true. I tried my best to block out the idea of him.

Even though nobody died at the prom, our notoriety lived on. But most of it was centered on me. Tonya seemed to fly beneath the radar, except when we were together. Then I was the Eric Harris and she the Dylan Klebold in the eyes of our classmates. Once our suspension ended, I was back to having people call me "psycho" between classes. Or they'd yell "boom" or "there's the school shooter girl." I followed my mom's advice for a week and a half, wearing pastels and going without makeup, but it didn't stop the harassment. It was too late. Walking around Spaulding felt like crossing the Red Sea now, the blood wave parting before me as I made my way down the long, drab hallways.

As far as I was concerned, the prom story was ongoing, since I was still experiencing the after-effects. So it was a shock, if a predictable one, when the news stories stopped. I missed the intensity, the electricity in the air. There'd been no climax or resolution. I was left high and dry, my status as pariah apparently set in stone, while the flattering attention had dwindled.

What did it mean? It had to mean something! I began to spend my lunch periods in the library looking through stacks of newspapers. I searched out stories of others across the country who were going through similar struggles. Reading about them made me feel less alone. I found pieces like an article called "Bomb Rumor Thins Attendance," which I pasted in the scrapbook where I kept track of the rumors about Tonya and me. The article, occasioned by a bomb threat at Deerfield Beach High School in Florida, included snippets about a rash of similar threats at schools around the state. On another page, I pasted a passage from Jon Katz's book *Geeks: How Two Lost Boys Rode the Internet Out of Idaho*[17]: "Since Littleton, the cost of being different has gone up. Thousands of powerful email messages have chronicled an educational system that glorifies the traditional and the normal, and brutalizes and alienates people who are or who are perceived as different under various names— geeks, freaks, nerds, Goths and oddballs [...] The hysteria over Littleton has only made things worse. It's time geeks defined and lobbied for some new rights."

Such rights appeared nowhere on the Barre horizon, so I tried to make the best of my outcast status. By May 19, I was writing in my journal: "I used to get stared at because of my clothes. But this is different. I can tell by the eyes. I have never received looks like this before by so many people. I'm not one to care about my reputation. I don't mind being a freak. But this is over the limit. In a way I like it. I know this is happening everywhere."

For better or worse, I was finally standing out. Once merely unpopular, I was now infamous. I could think of myself as the anti-prom queen.

Another scrapbook item is a local op ed from early in June, "Students React to Columbine." The piece focuses on rumors of school violence all over Vermont, including the line, "There were also rumors that someone would die at the Spaulding junior prom." I was indignant at this further confirmation of something I'd already noticed: news outlets frequently seemed unable to keep their facts straight or even get a grip on the story they were telling. Was it only one person who was supposed to die, or was it a group of students? Despite my position at the center of all the rumors, I myself didn't feel that I really understood what was going on, so how could these reporters and commentators? Before this, I'd never questioned the factual basis of what got presented as "news" in the papers or on TV. Now it struck me as shaky, maybe unreliable. I scorned "the media" for getting my story wrong, but even as I did so, I loved the attention. Before too long, I'd join "the media" myself, but of course I had no clue about that at the time.

My brush with infamy was a tiny taste of what it's like to be vilified in the media—the ultimate reward for serious plotters of mass shootings. I've noticed that this central motivation is often poorly understood; in fact, not only the general public but many news editors and producers haven't realized that mass shooters are an entirely different species of menace from serial killers. Both crave attention, but serial killers relish the act of killing while mass shooters typically distance themselves from their victims both physically (given the range of their weapons) and emotionally. At the center of their suicidal mission, instead, is anticipation of posthumous infamy.

An FBI report released in 2014 examined 160 "active shooter incidents" that took place between 2000 and 2013. The authors conclude that a goal of the perpetrators was to achieve notoriety. In view of this, the Bureau has supported a series of campaigns with names like "No Notoriety" and "Don't Name Them." That approach seems promising in light of positive results from a similar approach to suicide prevention. In the 1980s, after a number of suicides were attributed to a contagious media effect, the Centers for Disease Control and Prevention issued voluntary guidelines for reporting on suicides. The guidelines have since caught on. In recent years, news outlets have begun to voluntarily minimize the amount of media exposure given to mass killers, also in an effort to save lives.

While the news media certainly should be encouraged to take common sense steps to minimize the danger that media coverage of spectacular violence may encourage its repetition, the fact remains that we just don't know enough about the broader picture of mass shooter sympathizers and copycat threats. How do these "thought crimes" and malevolent pranks relate to the sordid, numbing reality of bloody mayhem repeatedly unleashed in schools, nightclubs, stores, houses of worship, and other ordinary settings throughout the U.S.? If there *is* a connection, what are we to make of many instances when, as in my case, identifying with media-hyped perpetrators is not the sign of a killer in the making, but a fantasy born of bewildered frustration with oppressive surroundings? In the course of my work as a reporter, I've had occasion to speak about this with academic experts as well as people with hands-on experience in law enforcement. I've spoken to current and former FBI agents as well as leading experts in gun violence and mass killings. I'm repeatedly amazed when they're unable to offer much in the way of authoritative, research-based insight. In fact, it turns out they don't claim to know anything beyond what I've managed to figure out through a combination of my own experiences and my research for stories.

James Hawdon, sociologist and director of the Center for Peace Studies and Violence Prevention at Virginia Tech, told me in 2021 that I'd need to gather data from the 18,000+ local law enforcement agencies to get such answers. Daniel Webster, director of the Center for Gun Policy and Research at John Hopkins University told me I wouldn't need to do that—a study with a sample population would suffice—but noted that this topic has received little funding. In fact, he noted that research into gun violence, or violence generally in America, receives a surprisingly low amount of funding and attention.

"When you look at the problem of violence generally in the United States, and its enormous social cost, and you look at federal or private funding for research on violence it is minuscule relative to the social costs," he told me in 2021.

With sympathy for the "devils" who unleash atrocious violence so weirdly prevalent, shouldn't it be a priority to study the issue?

CHAPTER 14

GOD COMPLEX

Maybe you've seen internet memes claiming that most mass shooters have one thing in common: antidepressants or other psychiatric drugs. Those memes don't lie. Eric Harris was on Luvox. Michael Carneal was supposedly on Ritalin. Kip Kinkel, who in 1998 murdered his parents before shooting up his Springfield, Oregon high school, killing two and wounding 22 others, was on both Prozac and Ritalin. Jeff Weise, a 16-year-old who shot and killed nine people and wounded five others before killing himself at his Minnesota high school in 2005, was on Prozac. Adam Lanza, who killed 26 at Sandy Hook Elementary School in 2013, was reportedly on anti-psychotics.[18]

In 2018, just two days after a massacre at the high school in Santa Fe, Texas, the National Rifle Association blamed Ritalin for school shootings, a move that naturally was not well received by gun control advocates. It seemed like both a cop out and a cynical distraction from the debate over restricting access to weapons. Some wondered why, if medication played a role, we weren't seeing a rash of female mass shooters; after all, one in five women is on a psychiatric drug, a rate more than double that of men.[19]

I soon joined the club of the medicated. The catalyst was my visit to the school therapist in fulfillment of the conditions my parents had agreed to in return for my being allowed to continue at Spaulding with a clean record. When I told this man I was tired of being harassed, he said that my peers were just blowing off steam. Their reactions were normal. So was Sarah's behavior in writing that note telling me what a slut I was.

I showed him the chat log between Sarah and Evan, the one in which she claimed I'd taken acid and hallucinated getting raped. I wanted to make him see that this wildly untrustworthy narrator was the same person who was responsible for the rumors that I was plotting mass murder. But once again, he seemed to find nothing abnormal in anything but me and my Elks Club story. Even when he walked me out after our session and heard kids taunting me with "Satanist" and "psycho," it didn't appear to faze him.

When I told my parents that I didn't want to keep seeing him, they arranged for a substitute: a psychiatrist who at least had the merit of not being connected with Spaulding. This was on top of a therapist I was already seeing at my parents' request.

The psychiatrist was young, in her late twenties or early thirties. From early in our session, I had a bad vibe.

"So," she began, "you suffer from depression?"

I said I didn't think so. "Maybe some anxiety. I have some racing thoughts."

She looked down at my black nail polish. It reminded me of a more polite version of some of my classmates' stares.

"Medication for depression could help with that, too. To me it's pretty clear you're depressed."

I started to tell her about what had happened with Sarah. "My best friend and I— we threatened a girl. My former best friend. She was bullying us. We weren't serious, we just wanted her to stop."

"Yeah," she said. "I read about that." She switched subjects in a way that let me know she didn't want to hear any more about the threat or the fallout from it. Maybe, I thought, it wasn't her job to hear it. But she looked uncomfortable, as though she was smelling something bad.

First, she put me on Luvox. I knew that Eric Harris had also been on Luvox and that some people thought this had been part of the problem. What if the drug pushed me closer to a choice like the one he'd made? Despite my worries, I went along with my parents' wishes. They'd come around to agreeing with the Spaulding officials that I needed to be on *something* in light of all that had happened.

On Luvox, I felt foggy during the day, but my dreams were extremely vivid. I didn't like the way they bled into my waking life. Returning to consciousness seemed to take longer than usual, and often it felt like I was hallucinating for a minute or two. Sometimes I'd wake up in the act of punching the wall. When I reported this, the psychiatrist switched me to Prozac. When that didn't end the hallucinations, she put me on Zoloft. Now at least I was no longer hallucinating, but Zoloft didn't lessen my anxiety. In fact, I felt more anxious than ever before, but numb and out of touch. It was like I'd been injected with emotional novocaine.

There is power in becoming the enemy, the other. Or at least in disguising oneself as such. Among non-human animals, it's a common defense mechanism. The puffer fish inflates to ward off predators, quickly ingesting water to fill its elastic stomach until it appears several times larger than usual. But an eye-catching appearance isn't always enough of a deterrent. Some of the most brightly colored, dramatic-looking animals on the planet are also the most deadly. The vibrant coral snake boasts more potent venom than all but one other variety of poisonous snake. The flamboyant cuttlefish is just that: flamboyant, and for a purpose. Often found off the coast of Australia, it sports a body that flashes rotating waves of color—magenta, orange, chocolate brown—almost like a computer screen. Its flashy presentation is a warning: don't eat me.

I hoped that with a human version of such tactics, I could be as successful at defending myself as these ingenious creatures. Perhaps a new, scarier persona would ward off the worst of the bullying. The rumors had handed me an opportunity; I would run with it. Behind the mask of my bravado, I nursed the fantasy that I was really powerful at a time when I had no power.

One night in early June, exactly one month after the school shooting rumors had peaked, I was writing in my journal. I sat on the floor, my faux fur zebra print rug beneath me. I could hear the crackle of thunder. As flash after flash lit up the walls of my room, a devious thought—really more of a fantasy—crossed my mind: I imagined the Elks Club getting hit by lighting. Or maybe the school. Or both. I had an impulse to "document" what I'd pictured occurring, so I wrote that I hoped lightning hit the Elks. Then I went to bed.

Next morning, I was taking a shower when my mom came and yelled through the bathroom door that school was cancelled that day. Spaulding had been hit by a lightning strike overnight.

"What?" I was dumbfounded.

"I heard it on the radio."

I stood there amazed with the water pouring down, not washing or even moving. School was never cancelled.

In my entire time in Barre, we'd never had a single snow day.

Tonya came over and it felt like a weird repeat of our out-of-school suspension the previous month. Like we were supposed to be in school, but something was off. We decided to go and scope out the building. On the drive there, I imagined finding some part of it blown to bits or scorched and blackened by fire.

When we pulled up, however, everything looked normal. Disappointingly normal. Disgustingly normal. We drove around the back parking lot under a sunny sky. On one of the back entrances, we spotted a piece of paper with a scribbled message. Three of our classmates were inspecting it.

We parked and went to see for ourselves. One of the students mumbled, "It was probably these two again."

The note said nothing more exciting than "School is cancelled for the day."

From the local paper, we learned that what the reporter referred to as a "well-placed bolt of lightning" had disabled the school building's alarm system. Fire fighters had arrived on the scene to find that most of the damage was confined to a portion of the library.

Intrigued by the idea of a well-placed lightning bolt, I started to fantasize that maybe my thoughts and wishes had had something to do with the unusual event. I connected it to a memory from the previous month: the Channel 3 news anchor declaring that a dark cloud of danger was hovering over prom night. Soon, Tonya and I became obsessed with lightning strikes. It was a month to the day from when we were accused of wanting to shoot up the school! I had never heard of lightning hitting Spaulding before. On the other hand, freak lightning strikes had happened in town before. A girl a few years older than me had been killed by one in the thick of a softball game. My brother's friend's mother was said to have lost her hair after being struck by lightning at her Spaulding graduation, held at an indoor venue away from the school. Despite this evidence that the whole thing could have been a coincidence, part of me believed—was eager to believe—that my wish and my journal entry had been the catalyst.

A few days later, I started my first job. The only place in town that seemed willing to hire me was Jockey Hollow Pizza, a crummy pizza and sandwich joint. I ran the cash, made sandwiches, mopped, and cleaned toilets. One of my coworkers, a woman in her late 40s with a husky voice and leathery skin, was also the mother of one of my classmates. I worried that she would figure out my identity as the girl at the epicenter of the rumors. At first she kept her distance, didn't say anything, but soon she made it clear that my reputation had followed me. I wrote in my journal: "Everyone in the whole town knows about the rumors. My supervisor at work finally told me today what she heard. She heard that I had a list of people alphabetically that explained what I wanted to do to each one and that it's five years old. Everyone who I think doesn't know just beats around the bush and says things like "'I loved the Elks Club dances from five years ago.'"

Five years ago, I'd locked eyes with Evan at one of those Elks Club dances. Now, after everything that had happened since Tonya scribbled that fateful note, it seemed all the more meaningful—like a memory tattooed on my skin instead of just a thing that I saw.

As the summer wore on, Tonya and I got braver. We began to fight back, albeit in immature ways. As I noted in my journal on July 1, Tonya was more assertive: "Other day in McDonald's Tammy Renold and some bitch and two pricks ran out when we walked in and said 'killer' so we chased after them and began screaming 'killer' and putting our hands up and Tonya said 'you got a problem with us?!?!' We then ACTED psycho. When someone calls me psycho, I'll be psycho alright. I'm sick of it plus it's FUN. I wanted to yell stuff too, but not yet." When our classmates got into their car and pulled out, I slowed to a jog, my boots clicking on the pavement. What an adrenaline rush. But once they drove off, I didn't know what to do with the leftover energy. Our target was gone, along with our audience. We just had ourselves.

My forlorn feeling had multiple roots. I was missing the chance of running into Evan that kept me going throughout the school year, but worse than that I was getting withdrawal pangs from being deprived of the fake relationship we'd had in my head. Before the note and all the rumors—"The Incident," as I now thought of it—I could at least believe there were glimmers of hope that he and I could have something: a friendship if not a romance. Now that seemed completely impossible.

The Incident infiltrated my dreams on an almost nightly basis. I recorded one in which I'd been driving my car when classmates began chasing me. I tried to get away, then stopped in the middle of the road. "I got out, picked up a baseball bat and smashed a hole in the air, which was made of glass, and hid under the road. Alicia chased me and asked if I wanted to fight and I said 'yes.' I recorded that we fought with our hands, but "I was frozen." In another dream; "Me and Tonya were at the Elks Club working in the bartender area. Then I watched the news in there and Evan's brother had died. I went down the hall and saw Evan laughing. I was blamed for the death."

Together, we watched both *Carrie 2: The Rage* and *Never Been Kissed*, movies released in the spring of 1999. While watching *Carrie*, I felt a mix of validation and jealousy when new Carrie's best friend Lisa died by suicide after jumping off the roof of the school. A a football had tricked her into thinking he cared for her, and she lost her virginity to him. It was a cruel joke that resulted in her being slut shamed and humiliated. I related to this character, as I did to Rachel, Carrie's predecessor. Lisa's fictional death reminded me of how I'd often fantasize about jumping off the roof of my middle school.   I felt it "my idea" when in reality I'm sure it was, and probably still is, a suicidal ideation of many troubled children. During *Never Been Kissed*, I had to hold back tears when Josie Geller was humiliated on her own prom night. In class she read out loud a poem she wrote about her popular crush Billy. In turn, he asked her out to their senior prom. On the night of the event, she dressed up in a 1980s dress. Madonna's "Like a Prayer" played, emphasizing her excitement as she waited for Billy to show up. When he did, another girl was with him in the limo, and they both hurled eggs at Josie as Billy told her to "write a poem about this, geek." One of the eggs struck Josie in the face and she crumbled to the ground bawling in pain. After the film's credits rolled, Tonya and I agreed that the film hit too close to home for the both of us.

When we watched *Summer of Sam* together, during the summer of 1999, I felt for Ritchie, a New Yorker who embraced the emerging punk scene by wearing a dog collar and engaging in counter culture. As the city struggled with mass hysteria during Son of Sam's 1977 killing spree, his neighbors began to suspect him as the killer, based on his appearance alone. This led to his brutal beating. The overinflation of fear caused seemingly normal people to panic, and turn on one another. I saw parallels between this and the post-Columbine vibes around me.

Apart from hanging out with Tonya, I had little social stimulation of either a positive or negative sort. I entertained myself as best I could. One sticky July night I watched live MTV footage of the Woodstock '99 festival as it went up in flames. In 1994, there'd been a successful re-creation of the famous Sixties gathering, but this one ended in a violent conflagration.

I wished I was there as Limp Bizkit's frontman, Fred Durst, exhorted a sea of shirtless white males not to mellow out. They responded by trashing the set. Some of them crowd surfed using pieces of plywood from the wreckage. The next night, fires broke out during the Red Hot Chili Peppers' set, their sound track a cover of Jimi Hendrix's "Fire." Intoxicated men began to mount a sound tower, which quickly collapsed. They looked to me like ants climbing a twig, weighing it down in the night as multiple fires blazed. After MTV pulled its crew out, the chaos continued. Trailers full of merchandise were stolen, vendor booths set ablaze.

At the time, I thought the whole thing looked dangerous but also exhilarating. It soon emerged that many were angry about conditions at the event. Water was expensive, days and nights were sweltering, shade was at a premium, and toilets inadequate. Nearly 500,000 people had shown up for what they hoped would be a peak experience sponsored by dozens of corporations.

I thought I recognized something in this new surge of anger. It was male, white, middle-class, and entitled—not unlike the spirit of the Columbine shooters. A part of me longed to be at the festival, to join in the chaos and feel the energy rush. But deep down, I knew I wouldn't have been able to do so. That world was for the boys, not me. The fires and riots weren't the end of the rebellion. At least four rapes were officially reported. One woman was said to have been gang raped during the Korn set, and another during Limp Bizkit's explosive set.

So how could I wield power? What would that look like? How could I exit my perennial role as victim without becoming a victimizer?

I often thought about all the verbal abuse I'd endured, years and years of it, starting in elementary school. Back then, Sarah had been targeted just as much as I was. It obviously required considerably more effort to mount that sustained assault than it took to scribble a menacing note and place it on a windshield. Why weren't our peers culpable for their endless barrage, all the times they'd called us whores and thrown literal garbage at us? They never got in trouble. Yet an impulsive, one-time act was met with harsh punishment.

Tonya and I went to a few witch events. The inspiration for this had something to do with *The Craft*, a 1996 movie I'd loved that focuses on a group of outcast teens who form a coven and begin casting spells. As their magic succeeds, they shed their lonely, insecure status. They become emboldened, even cocky. I wished that I, too, could gain confidence and exercise control by supernatural means. If lightning had struck Spaulding, what else might be possible?

As the end of summer approached and with it the start of school, Tonya and I sat smoking on her back porch. The night was clear and full of stars. I stared at the Big Dipper, exhaled luxuriously, and made an announcement: "I'm gonna start senior year with a different approach: with a God Complex!" What I meant was that I fully intended to get rid of everything meek about myself. At this point, why did it matter what anyone thought? I would own the rumors, responding with defiance. I'd put on an even more intimidating front. It wasn't even just a question of dressing how I wanted; I would wear the most outlandish things I could find, just to fuck with people.

Tonya laughed. "Me too," she said. "When I'm around you, at least. That's when people seem to recognize me."

I felt honored that my friend was so loyal. Tonya stuck by me even though she didn't have to. Despite the fact that we'd gotten into this mess together, we both knew that things could have worked out for her if she'd distanced herself from me.

CHAPTER 15

DEAD PROM QUEENS

Senior year began. My "God Complex" raged, but inside I felt like I was caving into myself. Eventually I would be able to put things in perspective, largely thanks to Mom's support. But right now, I couldn't see beyond my immediate circumstances. What kind of future was there for a misfit like me? Because I couldn't form a picture of any world beyond high school, the countdown to leaving Spaulding felt like The End.

On the first day of school, as I mounted the granite steps, I'd noticed that a girl I didn't know appeared to be scowling at me. I wondered why she didn't go in. Was she waiting to tell me I was a freak, a psycho? Startled, I discovered she was holding the door for me.

I thanked her. She said I was welcome. We exchanged smiles. Then I walked past a group of boys dressed in khaki—seniors, like I was.

"Wow, I can't believe Gina's still enrolled here."

"She's either insane or she has some major balls."

"I vote for insane. Makes sense. It's those quiet ones you gotta look out for."

That wasn't so bad, I thought. They weren't calling me names yet. I could even feel flattered by the fact that they gave me credit for being bold.

I went to my first class: Community Service Learning, taught by Ms. Scharf. In part, yes, I was taking that class because I wanted to do something positive in the community. At the same time, I wanted my old mentor to see that I wasn't crazy. I needed her to give me a chance. Secretly, I hoped she'd revert to the role she played in the days when I, a mousy-haired middle school kid, had been thrilled to have her call me a talented writer.

I lingered after class, hoping to talk one-on-one. She wouldn't look at me. When I approached, she walked out of the classroom.

Later that afternoon, I got a call from Krystal, who reported overhearing Ms. Scharf telling another teacher how upset she was at having me in her class. She said she couldn't imagine what community site would agree to take me on. Hearing this was a major blow. It wasn't that I hadn't already thought about the problems I might have trying to find a community placement, but Ms. Scharf's comment, plus the fact that she apparently intended to avoid me, made the whole situation feel impossible. I realized I would have to drop the class. Now I had an empty block in my schedule, a gap I needed to fill in order to graduate.

I made an appointment to see my guidance counselor, a brown-haired woman with a gentle demeanor that came across to me as inauthentic. In fact, she always reminded me of the gym teacher in *Carrie,* the one Carrie crushes with a basketball goal post. My plan was to transfer into the printing press and television production class in the vocational center, which Tonya had reported was easy and fun. Instead of letting me make the switch with a minimum of fuss, she expressed surprise that I was still enrolled at Spaulding due to The Incident. She said if she were me, she would have left the school. I explained that I had no desire to leave, even though my mom had encouraged the idea. It would seem like I was admitting guilt.

What I *did* feel, though I fortunately didn't say so, was more and more like Stephen King's anti-heroine. Though I understood that there were people at Spaulding, and probably many of them, who didn't think I was a potential murderer, I just couldn't get them in focus, any more than Carrie could contemplate the possibility of allies after having her coronation as Prom Queen implode in a shower of pig's blood. By this point I didn't even see Sarah anymore, barely physically in the halls nor in my mind; my anger towards her had been replaced towards general anger at the collective school.

This made me feel closer to how real school shooters must have felt, I figured and so I grew increasingly attracted to music genres and clothing that I connected with the Columbine killers. For example, I became a rabid fan of the band KMFDM. I already owned some of their music, but now I bought half a dozen more CDs and listened to them on repeat. I'd doodle quotes from their lyrics onto my binders. One favorite was from the song "Megalomaniac": "In the age of super-boredom,/Hype and mediocrity,/Celebrate relentlessness,/Menace to society." I also enjoyed "Godlike," where the singer Sascha seethes the words, "Pray, pray that your country undergoes recovery." I'd listen to KDFDM's "Vogue" repeatedly because I loved the intensity of the guitar riff when lead singer Sascha Konietzko sang "can you govern your soul?"

I became obsessed with the character Alex in Anthony Burgess's novel and the subsequent Stanley Kubrick film *A Clockwork Orange*. The fact that Alex and his "droogs" had their own private language made me think of my Elks Club book. I bought fake eyelashes that I sometimes wore on just one eye, copying Alex. My overall presentation became so extreme that this quirk barely registered with my peers. My dog collars got wider and spikier, my short skirts shorter, my fishnets more aggressively ripped. More black lipstick, more outrageously baggy pants. The new persona seemed to be working, at least to the extent that it allowed me to jump out of my spiky shell and make a scene.

As the rumors about my murderous propensities died down, I continued to chase the rush from The Incident. Tonya did too, I could tell. The two of us joined yearbook club but barely attended any meetings. Our only interest in the project was getting more pictures of ourselves into the yearbook so we could "leave our mark" behind. We caused trouble every chance we got.

I was allowed to transfer into the vocational class, which met in a basement corner of the school near an auto shop where kids spent the period learning to repair cars. At least I got to be with Tonya. Both Evan and Todd, the boy I'd hooked up with, were taking that class, but dropped it when I showed up. At parent-teacher night, my teacher reinforced my conviction that my enemies were many and well- organized. I wrote in my journal: "I'm so upset. Today Mr. Fogle told my parents about how some teachers told him shit about me. When I tried to sign up for his class they were like, 'You don't know what you are getting yourself into' and that I'm mentally ill. Teachers are no better than the students. Mr. Fogle didn't listen to it, thankfully. He said I was his best student in the class. Which makes sense because nobody else cares at all. I just want to get through this year without any shit but I also want my revenge."

What kind of revenge was I referring to? I don't think I even knew. I was wading through muddy emotional waters in my knee-high combat boots with the three-inch platform soles, the look that so disturbed and entranced my peers. Sometimes I wondered if I was capable of an act of violent revenge. Maybe so, but probably not. I felt less certain now than I remembered being in the days after Tonya left that note on Sarah's windshield.

In addition to her chat with Mr. Fogle, my mom had talked to Ms. Scharf on parent-teacher night. She wouldn't reveal all the details of what was said, but she told me, "Gina, once you graduate I give you permission to tell Ms. Scharf to go fuck herself."

I continued to do well in Mr. Fogle's class. He and a co-teacher recommended me for an after school job working at the local public access TV station. I'd be making graphics and transferring film to video. It didn't pay much but it felt like a real job, much better than cleaning toilets and mixing fresh mayonnaise together with crusty old mayonnaise at the pizza place. My bosses liked my work. And I got to hide out in a dark control room, away from the public.

I began to consider a career in television or film. As I saw it, the field was creative and had the potential to involve writing. I didn't think I had what it took to be a Writer per se, but I liked the idea of tackling something with a writing component. I knew I wanted a job I could be passionate about, but up until now I'd never been sure what would fit that description. Obviously I *was* a passionate collector of newspaper clippings about school shooting threats and rumors of violence. I felt I had a lot to say on the subject—more insight, in fact, than most of the journalists who were paid to cover it—but it hadn't been clear to me how that could translate into a college major, let alone a profession. Now it occurred to me that becoming a screenwriter or film director might open a path to my goal.

For fun, I even wrote part of a screenplay. Like everything else in my mind at the time, it focused on school shootings and took inspiration from the events of the previous spring. It centered on a girl who planned to commit suicide but first spent a year and a half building her own gun out of common household products. I can't say that I had any particular message in mind; I simply wanted to create fodder for controversy. At the same time, I relished the absurdist overtones. Why would a person who's dead set on death spend all that time constructing the means to their end? Tonya also relished the dark humor involved. We constantly joked about it.

My nights, as well as my days, still reflected my obsession. In the second half of October, I wrote: "The post Columbine shit will never end. I had another dream about   it. I went to a Halloween party at SHS. We all sat in a circle, and this trenchcoat guy pulled a sawed off shotgun out and began shooting paint. Everyone ran and started punching each other in (the back of) a pickup truck. Then the police came and everyone smiled. I went to a Barre Town Elementary School bonfire party. I read the newspaper and it said, "Ann Tron, Gina Tron's mom, said this about the incident..."

As Halloween approached, Tonya and I debated what to do. I wanted to dress up. My friend was skeptical.

"Where would we even go? Fuckin' Price Chopper?"

Why not, I wondered. "It's our hangout spot. I hope we run into some assholes while we're out."

We settled on dressing as dead prom queens. I wore my blue velvet junior prom dress, topped off with a sash my grandma had made with the words "PROM QUEEN" executed in glitter. I armed myself with a sparkly purple water gun and used makeup to create a fake bullet hole in my forehead. Tonya and I spent a half hour or so hanging out with our pseudo-friend Krystal, the one who usually avoided being seen with us in public. When she left for a party with some of our classmates, we headed over to

Price Chopper. I walked the aisles with my head held high, daring the shoppers to glance in my direction. Then I'd meet their eyes until they had to look down. I loved seeing how they reacted to us, with curiosity and fear.

As Tonya and I continued to chase the residual high from The Incident, we wrote something that came very close to getting us banned from *another* dance. It all started with an assignment: for our vocational class, we had to make a one-color poster. I used a photograph of myself in costume, pointing my water gun at Krystal. Both of us were smiling. I wrote some accompanying text: a headline that said "Barre Teen Attacked By Crazed Mental Patient," followed by the words, "Krystal Barkley, 17, was viciously attacked by the infamous Gina Tron, a longtime patient of the Spaulding Mental Institute here in Barre. The Spaulding Mental Institute is headed by Dr. Chip Anderson who said that Tron was on her daily dose of LSD when she ran away from the Institute and attacked Krystal. The Institute has regained control of Tron and now has her restrained and placed in a special solitary room in the basement of the Institute. Barkley sustained major injuries during the thirty second battle and was rushed to the hospital. Doctors say that she will probably pass away later on tonight."

Given everything that had happened, it was clearly provocative; the veil of parody did little to disguise my anger at the school and our insufficiently loyal friend. Still, I thought that Krystal would take it in good humor. Just a few months earlier, she and Tonya had celebrated my 17th birthday by "kidnapping" me with Mom's permission and assistance. Wearing masks and bandannas, they rushed into my bedroom, tied me up, blindfolded me, and threw me into the back of Krystal's Jeep. They drove me to Burlington and I laughed all the way, knowing that the stunt was modeled on *Jawbreaker,* the film in which a clique of mean girls kidnap their friend on her birthday and end up murdering her. I loved this film, as Krystal knew very well. I thought her appreciation of my dark sense of humor would mean that she wouldn't be bothered by the poster. By this point too, she had hooked up with Todd behind my back and seemed to find no issue with the way he treated me in the past. I put up with this because I knew friends could do worse but there was definitely some unresolved feelings of betrayal on my part.

But we made a second poster, and it was indeed much worse. It said: "Krystal Barkley: 1982-2000. She was killed by a demon named Gina and God above now sings with her angelic voice." In retrospect, it's plain we were invoking Columbine vibes, though I don't think we acknowledged it at the time.

We hung the posters up near one of Krystal's classrooms, which happened to be in the vicinity of the Community Service Learning classroom. Ms. Scharf spotted them and took them down to the office. She claimed to be offended and said that I was a menace. Krystal wasn't scared but she was angry at both of us. She told us that Ms. Scharf had said the posters confirmed what she already suspected. I was playing right into Ms. Scharf's warped image of me.

When Mrs. Minart called us down to her office, we feared it would be a repeat of the year before. It was just days before the Crystal Ball, an annual formal dance that was open to students from all grades. Tonya and I planned to go as each other's "dates"; really, we just wanted to dress up. There aren't too many occasions to do that in Vermont. In addition, making an appearance at the dance fit in with our policy of showing we weren't defeated. Whenever possible, we wanted to demonstrate our refusal to be forgotten or left out. If that took forcing our way into school functions where we weren't welcome, so be it.

Looking forward to the occasion, I'd bought a sleeveless silver mini-dress at a vintage store in Burlington. It was backless except for a criss-cross arrangement of thin black stripes. When the light hit the fabric, it threw off sparkles, almost like a disco ball. To go with the dress, I'd gotten six inch platform shoes, black and covered in glitter.

Mrs. Minart expressed concern that our posters might touch off more rumors about our wanting to do something bad at the dance. We told her that the thought hadn't occurred to us. And what we said was true. Though we were acting out our anger about The Incident, we hadn't been consciously courting its repetition.

Mrs. Minart said she understood. "Look, I get it, you guys. Last year was fucked up and I'm sorry."

My eyes widened. Stunned, I leaned back in my seat.

"But," she continued, "you can't do stuff like this. I get why you're doing it. Believe me, I do. But you can't keep doing things that people will use against you. You gotta be good. I know you girls are good."

Tonya voiced our appreciation for that last sentiment.

"But," Mrs. Minart continued, "parents are very weary of you. Teachers, too, to be honest. A big topic at the last PTA meeting was whether the two of you could be banned from the dances."

Tonya asked why. "Is this before the posters?"

"Yes. That's the problem. There wasn't a disciplinary reason for you to be banned. That's why you weren't. Now, there is." On the desk in front of her lay a copy of one of our posters. She jabbed a thumb at it. Her point was hard to argue with.

"But, I'm in *your* corner," she concluded. "Just try to keep a low profile."

Her words melted me. "Okay, I'm sorry."

I meant it, but wasn't sure how—or if—I could fulfill her request. At this point, really, how could I help myself? There were strands of gray in her dark hair now; they hadn't been there the year before. Within weeks of our conversation she resigned from her job, and I never knew the reason. It probably had nothing to do with Tonya and me, but I can't help thinking that whatever her troubles, we must have added to them. Later, my parents mentioned having heard that she'd had a nervous breakdown while trying to deal with Spaulding's crisis—*our* crisis—the previous spring. There was no way to gauge our degree of responsibility, if any—supposing the story had any truth to it. There's nothing to prove it wasn't just another rumor, as baseless as the one about our plot to hide a bomb in the popcorn machine.

Mrs. Minart's fear that the posters would touch off another frenzy wasn't borne out. Tonya and I attended the dance as planned. I wore a long coat in mauve velvet over my silver dress. I can't remember what Tonya wore, although her tastes at the time would have run to something long and black and elegant. Upon entering the venue—not the Elks Club this time—we went to the bathroom for a look in the mirror. Emerging from one of the stalls, a girl from a lower grade told us we looked nice, and we returned the compliment. My hopes rose that the evening might unfold without any nasty incidents.

On to a ballroom festooned with gold and black balloon arches. By now I'd taken off my coat, and my silver outfit made a splash, but not the kind I wanted.

"Whoa! Crazy! Look at psycho's dress!"

I turned to my friend. "What the fuck are they talking about?" Compared to the outfits I often chose for their shock value, there was nothing "crazy" about my dress.

Tonya agreed with me. I eyed all the eyes on us as we moved through the crowd. From across the room I spotted Jennifer, a popular senior girl in a shiny dress impossible to ignore. The back was a little less revealing than mine, but essentially we were wearing twin outfits—only hers wasn't causing any commotion.

People were laughing, and staring, pointing, and contorting their face with looks of disgust as they looked me up and down.

"Do you want to get out of here?" Swept by the flashing purple lights, Tonya's face looked distorted.

"Yes, we made our appearance."

As we retreated, I flipped off someone who made another nasty comment. At the door, Tonya swiveled and flipped off everyone. Laughing, we ran out of the building, heels clomping like galloping ponies, snow falling hard towards us through the black sky. Shivering, we slowed to a walk, denouncing our asshole classmates on the way. As far as we were concerned, they were all total jerks. We'd completely forgotten the nice girl in the bathroom.

Tonya started her old clunker and hit the gas. Laughing, she screeched the tires and leaned on the horn that sounded like a dying duck. I rolled down my window, stuck my middle finger out, and yelled "Fuck you" at the people clustered outside the entrance. I didn't care that I had no idea whether that bunch of kids included any of the ones who'd been making fun of us. They were all lumped together in my mind at this point, a blur of jerky peers I'd never be able to relate to. How did they get to be so comfortable, with dates and other normal high school experiences—all the things I'd imagined would be mine at this age?

Senior year wore on, a monotonous blob. I no longer had my Evan fantasy to fall back on. I'd lost my desire to write. Was it just the prescription drugs I was taking that made it feel like our English class spent months watching clips from a film adaptation of *Wuthering Heights?* Physics was boring, too, but stood out because of the fact that when assignments required writing our names up on the blackboard, my classmates took to designating me as "Elka." When that happened, I'd always check to see if people were confused, but they accepted it calmly. Given the fact that my screen name was xELKAx666, I shouldn't have been shocked, but the whole thing made me think of the Elks Club book and that tore me up inside. Even though I'd approached writing that story as an elaborate joke, it had meant a lot to me, and having it demonized felt like a piece of my core was being ripped out. What I wanted to write, what I wanted to do, who I wanted to be—I was getting the message that all of it was just too weird for me to lovable. And the only love I was getting was in the form of harassment and even strange death threats. I arrived home from Tonya's one night to my brother relaying a message from an unidentified male caller.

"Tell Gina I love her, and that I'm going to kill her," they apparently said. Again.

My friendship with Tonya was one of the few things in my life that offered any sense of connection. But we didn't share a lunch period, and since I didn't like the idea of braving the cafeteria alone, I just drove around smoking cigarettes in Mom's old Toyota Corolla, which I'd inherited. After so many years of being a passenger, at least I finally had my driver's license.

One Sunday I was lounging in my room, watching the movie *Heathers,* dressed in black baggy pants and a Nine Inch Nails tee. On the screen, Veronica (played by Winona Rider) wore a gray cardigan with shoulder pads as she chased her classmates through the woods. She was armed with a small handgun that her trench coat wearing boyfriend had informed her was loaded with "ich luge bullets," i.e. bullets that don't actually kill people. ("Ich luge" means "I'm lying" in German.)

Mom stuck her head in the door, saying we had to talk about my college applications.

"Don't you knock?"

"Gina, attitude check." She walked in and sat on my bed. I pressed pause, freezing the movie on Christian Slater in a trench coat.

"Mom, I don't even know if I want to go to college."

"You *have* to. You *have* to get out of here. Trust me, Gina, you're going to fit in much better in a more urban environment."

I expressed my skepticism, even though I certainly couldn't imagine a promising career in the local community. While I liked the prospect of working in media or film, I hated the thought of wasting four more years in an educational setting. I'd had enough of school— period.

"I'm not going to let you not go to college."

"I hate school! I'll be 18 soon. Then I can do whatever I want!"

I stormed out of my room, grabbed my keys, and drove down the hill into the heart of Barre City, Rob Zombie's "Living Dead Girl" blasting from my speakers.

As I approached an intersection, the red light turned green. I hung a quick left.

BANG. I smashed right into an oncoming car, T-boning it. In the shock that followed the impact, my instinct wasn't to check on anyone's welfare—not that of the other driver, nor even my own. Instead, I felt acute embarrassment that "Crawl on me, sink into me" was still screaming from my speakers. I quickly turned down the volume, hoping nobody would notice.

I got out and surveyed the wreckage. I could see that the driver of the car I'd hit was a boy who'd been in the class ahead of me and had recently graduated. His girlfriend, a sophomore, was the only passenger.

"I'm so sorry!" I began.

"Are you all right?"

"Yeah. Are you guys?" My answer was the sight of the girl in the passenger seat rubbing the back of her neck. There was nothing I could do, but as I stood there in the middle of the increasing traffic pileup, I desperately wished I could go back in time and take that turn more carefully. A lot more carefully.

Traffic was blocked in three directions from the town's main intersection. Among the inconvenienced were a few of my classmates, one of whom yelled "psycho" from his open window. The worst of it was knowing I couldn't blame anybody else. The other driver had had the right of way and I'd failed to yield. Not yielding had become a way of life for me, but unlike with Sarah or the school or even my mom, in this case I really couldn't claim it as a virtue.

I walked back to my car and sat with the door open, waiting for the police to arrive. Suddenly, a middle-aged woman with a gentle smile knelt on the ground beside me.

She put a hand on my knee. "It's okay. These things happen." She grabbed my forearm and squeezed it.

"Thank you," I mouthed over the racket of sirens approaching.

On the police report, I admitted fault for the accident, once again setting down on paper a bunch of words that would end up causing me years of trouble, this time in the form of drastically higher insurance rates. After the tow truck left with my car, I waited on the sidewalk for my parents to collect me, exposed to the stares of every passing classmate.

I sat in the back seat as my dad drove us home. Mom turned around and glared from the passenger side. "Why did you write that?"

"You taught me not to lie."

"What else did I teach you? If it involves the police, you gotta shut up!"

My Toyota Corolla was totaled. When I returned to school on Monday, "Get in any car accidents lately?" was a popular line. I overheard grumbling that I must have purposely caused the crash to hurt people who'd made fun of me. The fact that even a car crash could be viewed as resulting from a sinister plan of mine briefly boosted my spirits despite the guilt I felt for my carelessness.

On a warmer night than usual for the season, we experienced a massive—I thought magnificent—lightning storm. I watched from our back porch as bolts of electrical energy tore across what had been a pitch black sky, lighting up the hilly range beyond the woods at the end of our property. The show fed my wildest fantasies that Tonya and I could tap into some method of unleashing hidden powers. Was it the right day of the month for weird shit to happen? Was the storm because of us?

Suddenly, I felt sick to my stomach and threw up over the edge of the deck. Recovering, I heard a strange sound. It sounded like a train, but there were no trains nearby, and I realized it was more like a choo-choo train, not a modern one. I turned my head toward the spot where our chicken coop stood, and realized, with the next lightning flash, that I couldn't see the coop because something large was blocking it. I gasped, now convinced that what I'd thought was a train in the distance actually was a noise made by an animal—a *creature*—breathing very close to me. In a panic, I rushed to get inside the house, fumbling with the deck's sliding door, then locking it behind me. I was screaming.

"Gina," Mom shouted, "what the hell's going on?"

"There's something out there! It was breathing!"

"It's probably just some kind of animal."

But I was convinced it was something supernatural. (Whatever it was, recalling that encounter still gives me chills.) Tonya and I discussed it, agreeing that lightning had a habit of striking around the 7th or 8th of each month. The phenomenon, we decided, had something to do with us. I wonder now if I was influencing her, just like I'd influenced people with the Elks Club book. On some subtle level, was I manipulating her? Of the two of us, I was still shyer when it came to speaking out. But everyone who believed the rumors about us thought that I was the leader and she was my accomplice.

I began having nightmares about lightning strikes. In a typical journal entry from late November, I wrote: "Last night I had another dream about lightning killing people, only instead of it being at prom this time it was inside the school. I heard people screaming while they were being killed, but there was also this horrible noise that sounded like the raptors from Jurassic Park."

For just long enough to record one studio album, some musicians from KMFDM broke off to create the industrial band MDFMK. Released on that 2000 album, their song "Witch Hunt" addresses the aftermath of the Columbine shootings. I listened to it over and over, the lyrics booming at me from my styrofoam headphones.

Bolts of lightning, out of the blue, without forewarning, the heat is on you.

The song might have been written expressly for me. Lightning. Post-Columbine hysteria. Stories of chaos, mayhem, and death.

Moral cleansing, free thinking must burn. This is serious, your face in the mud. The end of the story is written in blood.

To me, the lyrics spoke of being featured in the news. Being tarred and feathered by the media.

It doesn't matter what you say or do. There is no justice, no future for you, because you're the scapegoat, you are to blame. This is your life: fifteen minutes of shame.

That was it, I thought: fifteen minutes. Fifteen minutes of notoriety in a tiny town was the outer limit of what I could aspire to in life. I had hopes for more, but little expectation. Maybe I'd never succeed at anything, but a turn in that shameful spotlight is better than nothing, right?

CHAPTER 16

MY FAVORITE SHOOTER

Here's something I've been embarrassed about for most of my life: in senior year, I joined an online message board for people obsessed with the Columbine killers. I felt aligned with them and wanted an outlet. To the best of my recollection, my thought process went: if Eric Harris and Dylan Klebold had been classmates of mine, they'd have understood the pain I was going through, and would never have ostracized me like my actual peer group did.

One hot topic on the message board was the buzz of anticipation surrounding the basement tapes. These were videotapes that the killers had made in hopes that they'd be widely available to the public. They wanted people like me, like us, to be inspired—not unlike other sorts of terrorists bent on recruitment. I began posting regularly on the message board and struck up a friendship with a Goth girl from Ireland. She felt connected to Dylan Klebold, whom she saw as deprived of love, a feeling she could definitely relate to. We exchanged physical addresses and she sent me a handwritten letter addressed to "Elka." In it, she included all sorts of details about how cute she thought her favorite shooter was. I agreed; at the time, I found him cute and alluring. I felt bonded to him and his friend because I saw them as victims—a notion I later vehemently discarded. Back then, I thought the people they shot were victims as well, but a different kind of victim, not the kind I identified with.

The letter from my pen pal included some photos of her. She sat in a verdant field wearing a loose-fitting black velvet dress, a scowl on her face, black circles setting off her baby blue eyes. She looked so cool, I wished she lived nearby. I hid the envelope and its contents at the bottom of a shoebox, under letters from my old friends on Long Island.

A few months later, I became paranoid and tore up the Irish girl's letter. I was scared that someone would find it and conclude that the rumors had been true, that I really had wanted to massacre my classmates. The fact was that despite my empathy for the kind of people I thought the Columbine killers were, I'd never believed their actions were right. I did wonder, though, if being pushed hard enough could make me capable of murdering my tormenters. On the other hand, if that were the case, shouldn't I have erupted by now?

I checked myself for homicidal urges but didn't discover any. I did have dreams in which I played the role of shooter, but always in the aftermath of slaughter. It was never me with a sawed off shotgun pumping rounds into people; instead, I was being interrogated about the murders I'd allegedly committed. I'd always be confused, because I couldn't remember them.

Eventually, by the end of senior year, I did start to have some fleeting fantasies of shooting up Spaulding, but I'd suppress them pretty fast. I thought that I was maybe capable of it, that possibly all humans have murderous violence in us, but I also knew that path just wasn't for me. This might have had something to do with the fact that all my pessimism about my future social life couldn't extinguish a spark of hope. I thought there had to be a world where I could find career success—even if, for the moment, I had no idea how to get there.

I had other fantasies too that were much more naive, of being popular but doing it right, moving up the social ladder while being kind. I'd often watch the ending of *Heathers* and smile. I loved when Veronica ripped the scrunchie (a symbol of power) out of her popular frenemy's hair and sternly said"there's a new sheriff in town," before befriending a badly bullied classmate.

Beyond the phenomenon of online fan sites like the message board I joined, there's a great deal of evidence suggesting that the fantasy of connecting with school shooters is widespread, among adolescent girls in particular. If anything, it has increased in the years since Columbine. For example, Nikolas Cruz, perpetrator of the infamous 2018 massacre that left 17 people dead at his Parkland, Florida high school, received stacks of fan mail and even love letters, many penned by teenage girls. One wrote, "I'm 18-years-old. I'm a senior in high school. When I saw you on television, something attracted me to you."[20]

Broward County Public Defender Howard Finkelstein, whose office represented Cruz, told a reporter for a local paper that the letters chilled him. Why? Because they were written by people he considered to be normal. "The letters shake me up because they are written by regular, everyday teenage girls from across the nation," he said. "That scares me. It's perverted."

Online groups that sprouted after the Parkland shooting included one called "Nikolas Cruz—The First Victim." This was a private group with hundreds of members, many of whom used hashtags like #StopBullying. Though in all likelihood some of these people do condone murder, I very much doubt that all of them do. I speculate that an important subset may entertain the same type of misguided empathy that I felt for the Columbine shooters. Despite evidence from studies that have found an absence of any obvious correlation between bullying and mass murder, the legend of such a connection remains powerful. Those who have been bullied have an extra incentive to invest in stories of shooters as heroic underdogs and girls in particular feel empathy for them. James Hawdon, a sociologist and director of the Center for Peace Studies and Violence Prevention at Virginia Tech, told me in 2021 that while males look to school shooters to identify and "learn" from them, females lean towards "understanding" and "empathizing" and "loving" them.

Despite the role that social media has played in offering a forum to fans of murders, the fandom itself is hardly a new phenomenon. Between the time that serial killer Ted Bundy was apprehended in 1978 and his execution in 1989, he received piles of fan mail and marriage proposals. Susan Klebold's memoir reveals that she was flooded with love letters for her son Dylan.[21]

Decades after Columbine, its legend lives on. "I care more about Eric and Dylan than I do about 90% of the people around me," a 17-year-old girl who goes by "reb420angel" posted on Tumblr. She was born in 1999, the year of the shootings. She's just one of many female admirers who continue to gather on social media, bonding over their fantasies of how cool, cute, and tormented the teenage killers were.

I've alluded to my fixation on the movie *Heathers,* a dark comedy from the late 80's that I watched on my VHS player at least once a week. It stars Winona Ryder as a popular girl gone rogue. She collaborates with a new kid —a loner boy in a trench coat—to off several classmates before realizing the error of her ways. In the end, she prevents her partner from unleashing a massacre. My favorite part was when the loner, J.D., talks about blowing up their school. I especially loved the lines, "People will look at the ashes of Westerburg and say, 'Now there's a school that self-destructed, not because society didn't care, but because the school was society.' Now that's deep." *School is society*—the formula rang true to me. It portended a life of hell for which I tried to prepare myself, urged on by my perception that the Barre adults were as bad as the kids. One small but telling example of this was reported by my mother after she went shopping for some item of winter gear, a jacket or a vest, at a locally owned store. The adult sales clerk recommended a specific brand and style by saying that it was the choice of a couple of high school athletes who were popular in town. She simply assumed that this would impress my mom, who was in her mid-40s at the time.

I finally gave in and applied to some colleges, not because I shared Mom's conviction about the importance of education, but because I agreed with her that I needed an urban environment. Or at least I hoped that I might do better there. Though I didn't feel assured of any positive outcome, I did know I needed to get the fuck out of Barre. When I pictured my social life in the new setting, I kept my expectations low. Best case, I might be able to make friends with a handful (maybe three?) of the college's weirdos. I thought maybe I'd find a weirdo boyfriend, shy and from a small town in some place like Alabama. He'd be a male version of me and we'd be inseparable. Sometimes I pictured him as being from Colorado, because basically I thought my only option for love would be a less homicidal version of the Columbine killers. During the summer before college, I spent a lot of time in my family's computer room, listening to KMFDM, researching Columbine, and fantasizing about   a life in Colorado. Suppose I'd met and dated Eric or Dylan—wasn't there a good chance they'd have been nicer than the crop of Spaulding boys?

I never shared these thoughts with Tonya, or confessed my participation in a fan site devoted to the killers. Instead, we continued to track lightning storms, excitedly speculating that they *had* to mean something. In a journal entry from March, 2000, I recorded: "Yesterday night, I was at Anya's and we heard thunder and we were like 'Yes!' It's the first time there's been lightning for months and it's on the 25th!!!!! 3 special days a month! 8, 20, 25." When lightning struck, it had planted an idea: apparently, a thunderbolt from on high had the potential to be as spectacularly disruptive as an act of mass murder, while conveniently avoiding any troubling moral questions.

CHAPTER 17

REAL PROM QUEEN

On April 17, 1999, just three days before the Columbine shootings, Dylan Klebold put on a traditional black tuxedo and got into a limousine. Accompanied by a date (just a friend, not a girlfriend) and a dozen other companions, he rode to his senior prom. His date was a girl named Robyn Anderson, who had been the middleman (or woman) in a "straw sale," procuring three of the four guns used in the massacre. She was later described as a sweet, Christian girl; she claimed she'd had no idea what Dylan and Eric were planning.

In the wake of the tragedy, Dylan's friends reported that he'd been in excellent spirits that night. They thought he seemed happy, optimistic even, about his future. I couldn't help thinking that he certainly had a better prom experience than I did, even if it was all a front for him. So what if he didn't fall in love at prom, slow dancing with his longtime crush in the light of a twinkling disco ball. At least he'd had a high-profile date with the opposite sex. That was something I never had in my high school years, despite all the movies that told me I deserved it. I would have killed, I thought (pun totally intended) to have a boy ask me to prom—even a friend I harbored no romantic feelings for.

Among the movies that helped me formulate my unrealistic picture of what this peak event ought to look like, *Pretty in Pink* stands out as one of the few where the weirdo girl ends up with the popular guy and not the other way around. The heroine, Andie, uses her sewing talents to design a uniquely expressive prom dress. On the fateful night, she scores a victory over her school's social hierarchy when Blane, the wealthy boy she's pining for, defies peer pressure to declare his love. The film ends with their passionate kiss. Over the years, this ending gave me hope that one day Evan would stop being cowed by the social dynamics of our stupid school.

But even back then, a part of me realized that while life may sometimes seem as *strange* as a film, it's a lot more nuanced, and with fewer happy endings.

As senior prom approached, I got increasingly anxious. Should I/we go? Would there be more drama? Considering what had happened at the Crystal Ball, it didn't seem farfetched to feel apprehensive that this last dance of my high school career would offer nothing more than a further opportunity to cement my status as outcast. By late March, I was writing in my journal that I didn't think I wanted to go to prom, that even going to the Elks Club for a school awards dinner made me feel humiliated *"because everyone knows that I am obsessed with that place."*

In the end, Tonya and I decided to go. Really, how could we bear to stay away? It seemed like we'd risk missing out on all the action. Besides, I was totally programmed to expect this dance to be the climax of the movie that was my teen life. As I found out later, the tradition of prom had started in elite university settings in the nineteenth century, supposedly to encourage "social etiquette." By the early 1900s, it was being adopted in high schools, and thirty years later was firmly entrenched there. Its popularity dipped during the Vietnam War, but revived with reinforcement from all the popular films I loved, including *Prom Night,* a 1980 slasher flick with multiple sequels throughout my birth decade.

No wonder I could have echoed the sentiment once voiced by a character from the TV show *Glee:* "Next to my wedding, my prom dress will be the most important gown I ever wear."

If junior prom had been eventful, senior prom ought to be more so, like a sequel that reveals further layers of meaning.

On an afternoon in May, I noted dramatically: "Perhaps this is my last entry. I'm going to prom 2 night. They really played it down this year—no announcements, posters. Only 2 things in the bulletin. I am gonna shock everyone with my dress. Everyone thinks I'm gonna go Goth. [A classmate] was like 'tell me what your dress looks like. I know it's gonna be black.' hahah no. I wonder if everyone is gonna get searched this year, like last year caz o' me.

"Last night I had a dream with all these police sirens and police cars. I think it was in a house but it was prom. Everyone was there. Evan was talking to me."

The big night got underway just as the sun was going down. Tonya and I posed for pictures at the edge of my family's driveway. Behind us, the sky was painted with various cotton candy colors, while the green mountains below took on unusual hues of their own. The pastel atmosphere seemed to match Tonya's baby yellow dress, with spaghetti straps revealing her clavicle and shoulders. Slightly puffy at the bottom, the skirt reached her ankles. I was wearing a two-piece dress from a vintage shop. The white tube top was decorated with baby blue rhinestones and trimmed with matching blue lace, while the iridescent blue skirt, long and high-waisted, was shaped like a mermaid's tail. I wore my hair in an updo, the ends of it colored blue with temporary dye and coiled in tight ringlets. The crowning touch was my dainty wire tiara, dotted with tiny rhinestones, a blue gem at its arch.

It was still dusk when we parked our car across from the Elks Club. As we approached the brick building, I could feel my heart beat fast. I thought about the scene in *Pretty in Pink* where Blane finally admits his love for Andie. I always thought her friend Duckie —such a goofy, stylish dork—would suit her a lot better than bland, preppy Blane. But that was a quibble; the main point, as I saw it, was that this is the effect that prom has on people. It lets them be bolder, better, lets their true selves emerge. Maybe someone would ask me to dance, I thought—and then, like a reflex, I pushed the thought aside. Before all the rumors, it might have been possible. Now, there was no way. The vision of what I'd lost felt almost unbearable, and I tightened my grip on my small silver purse. My mom had given it to me; it was studded with shiny sequins. The surface gleamed like a reticular disco ball.

Tonya and I got plastic cups of pink punch and sat down at a table in the corner. The principal, who'd never said a single word to us at the time of The Incident, decided it was time to sit with us and strike up a friendly conversation—probably wanting to stage that he was monitoring us and had everything under control. That's what I thought then, anyway, and it's what I think now.

With a big smile, he asked, "How are you ladies doing?"

"Fine," we mumbled.

"Stayin' out of trouble?" he joked.

I smiled awkwardly. Maybe I even laughed. I glanced around to see if people were watching, but hardly anyone seemed to have noticed. Soon, the man got up and left us alone. Everything felt too calm, too dull. I snapped a picture of a police officer who wandered onto the dance floor at one point, but that was the only hint of any security concerns.

As the evening wore on, my confidence rebounded, and I started telling people to vote for me for prom queen. I figured I was Spaulding's Carrie White, so it was only appropriate. Winning prom queen would be meta, it would be a laugh riot. At some point, I got high enough on this notion to drag Tonya out on the dance floor under the spinning disco ball.

"We have to dance," I told her. "Once, at least!"

At first she didn't look happy, but then we both cut loose, acting silly, dancing our way toward the stage. They were playing A Teen's version of ABBA's "Dancing Queen," and I sang along in a shrill, high voice as we flailed our arms wildly.

From the stage, a photographer yelled for everyone to pose together. "We gotta make *the* face!" I told Tonya. We tried to assume a scary, sulky pose, staring down the long, black camera lens, while the others around and behind us grinned as hard as they could. In the picture that resulted, we appear at center left, apparently further forward than all the rest. Tonya's brow is dark and furrowed, and both of our heads are lowered. We appear just as we wanted— miserable, menacing—while our peers reproach us with their happy masks.

After we'd posed for that photo, I felt emboldened, thrilled that we'd be leaving our mark on the yearbook. Glowing with the thought that we'd be remembered even if most of our classmates preferred to forget us, I walked right up to a classmate, looked her in the eye, and told her to cast her vote for me as prom queen. Then I did the same to a bunch of other people. Some reacted with shock that I was talking at all, and when they heard what

I had to say emitted brief bursts of laughter like a balloon being deflated.

Tonya and I went back to our corner table and scribbled "Elka and Anya" on the tablecloth: leaving our mark again. Bored, we talked about leaving, but decided to wait and find out who had been chosen prom queen— just in case it was time for my big *Carrie* moment, we joked.

And then the atmosphere shifted. "Something seems to be up," Tonya said.

I looked up from staring at my silver purse, whose multitude of sequins resembled flashing fish scales, their colors constantly shifting in tandem with the rotating lights on the dance floor. Some of the more popular girls huddled anxiously near the table where the ballots were being counted. A few of them were looking my way.

"What now?" I wondered.

"Maybe more rumors? Are the cops gonna yank us out?"

"Why is Jen crying?"

A girl in a peach-colored dress, her red hair up in a French braid dotted with tiny paper roses, came over and spoke to me. "I think you won prom queen! There's a big stack of ballots with your name on them. They're trying to figure out what to do."

Tonya and I grinned as the girl rushed back to the ballot table. "Oh my God, Tonya. What should I say if I win? Will I get to make a speech like in the movies?"

She insisted we had to come up with something funny for me to say. We waited for the announcement while discussing various options. The whole situation felt preposterous—but it was happening. Classmates began to stand up. They clustered on the dance floor and moved towards the stage. Tonya and I followed at the back of the pack. I couldn't see over the heads in front of me, had no idea who was talking or what was being said. I flashed back to how I'd felt at the sixth grade Elks Club dance, tiny and overwhelmed by all the bigger people.

An audible announcement ended the suspense. "And the Prom Queen is Lizzy Black."

Her ballot pile must have been thicker than mine. I turned to Tonya.

"Fuck this," she consoled. "Let's blow this joint."

I laughed angrily. "Don't say that too loud. Next thing you know we'll be in handcuffs."

We walked out of the Elks Club past a blur of faces. Outside, the night was still and summery. We headed to McDonald's for a compensatory treat. According to photos we took there, I'd changed my long skirt for a pair of faux snakeskin leggings, but I kept the crop top on. I ordered a chocolate fudge sundae and dribbled some of my ice cream over the smooth purple crotch of the Grimace on a placemat. (Spoiler: it was supposed to be semen.)

Despite our bravado in the moment, I felt sad when I got back home. Though it might seem obvious that a person like me—shy and awkward to begin with, now with her reputation torched— shouldn't expect a whole lot from prom, I couldn't help feeling wounded by the fact that *two* proms had gone by and I'd never had a slow dance, let alone a kiss. Even Dylan Klebold had a better prom than me! I felt ripped off. In my journal, I recorded my satisfaction at having persuaded a lot of people to vote for me.

Much later, it emerged that I actually *did* win. Confirmation came during our ten year class reunion which, like many of the other school functions I attended in connection with Spaulding, I mostly went to out of spite and defiance. Called Senior Prom Redux, it was held at the Elks Club, and that further fueled my disdain and desire to go. It was shortly after attending that event, which long-story short didn't go well, that a class officer herself admitted having intervened with the prom queen decision. She said that a lot of people had voted for me "as a joke." When I ended up winning, she'd told the ballot counters to announce that those in second place had won king and queen. She didn't say who'd gotten the most votes for king, and I didn't think to ask, but it was probably Tonya. This prom queen "win" was apparently discussed as soon as I entered the Elks Club in 2010 for my reunion. It got back to me and it prompted my questioning of the 2000-themed event.

The belated clarification came as no surprise, given rumors I'd heard back in high school. In response to them, I bought a tee that said THE REAL PROM QUEEN. When I wore it to school, I sometimes got positive feedback from classmates who otherwise never talked to me. "Hey, that's pretty funny. Not gonna lie!" They'd smile genuinely and I'd smile back.

A journal entry from this time shows me straining for closure: "I AM THE REAL PROM QUEEN and I always will be. Wink Wink. I was on EVERYONE's Mind during Junior Prom and this year I pissed some people off. Junior year I was queen of Elks Club, I took it over, made news, everyone knew about my book, rumors I would shoot it up. This year, I proved to everyone I could go to prom. MISSION ACCOMPLISHED. I will now stop talking about this incident."

Well, that didn't really work out as planned, did it?

In the aftermath of prom, I still clung to hope that I could exit the hell of high school with a metaphorical bang. Predictably, it turned out to be a sputter.

I used Angelfire, a website-building platform popular at the time, to create my own web page. I posted files of a few songs I liked, and I also used the venue as a sort of public journal, a chance to vent my ongoing frustration at being the object of gossip and nasty comments. "There is not one week where I don't get yelled at by a random person, or overhear or have my friend overhear someone saying stuff like how I wanted to blow up the school...Well I never wanted to blow up the school or shoot anyone, so, ahh! [...] Sometimes I like to pretend that people forgot all about it, or that they know the truth. But then I find out I am wrong like whenever I go out in public. But I really am a nonviolent person. Besides why would I do something like that? Sure, I get pissed off at people who harass me, but I'm not going to destroy my life just to get back at a bunch of assholes. It's not worth it!"

Tonya and I decided to skip an event called "Project Grad," a massive post-graduation party that we figured would just recycle all the uncomfortable dynamics of prom. We did go to graduation, though. I thought of a cheap, sparkly way to jazz up the sobriety of the traditional cap and gown. Starting with a plastic tiara studded with clear rhinestones and a fuchsia heart gem, I cut off the plastic grooves and glued what remained onto the top of my cap. To this I added a three-line message in black letters on white paper:

I'd like to thank God
Oh wait

I AM GOD

It still embarrasses me to admit that I was somewhat inspired by Eric Harris's habit of signing his classmates' yearbooks with the line "Ich Bin Gott." (As for my own yearbook, only Tonya and Krystal signed it, and even Krystal's signature felt like a concession, since our friendship had never recovered from the poster incident.)

I'd recently dyed my hair pink and purple—straight up My Little Pony colors—and the blue and red strings of the tassel on my cap blended with my pinkish blond hair. I wore that cap boldly, owning its message of defiance, keeping my shoulders back as my class walked in file. I was determined not to flinch under the stares from the audience. Unsurprisingly, some parents were offended, and so were a few of my peers. I overheard one girl, someone who'd reportedly been upset about the prom queen debacle, complaining to her friends that my getup was disrespectful. As it was, of course, but so many disrespectful things went down at Spaulding. My cap was hardly the worst of it, I thought. Besides, who cared at a moment when we were all supposed to be moving past the bubble of high school? Given that the authorities (adults, Hollywood) constantly talked about high school as the best time in a person's whole life, it seemed to me that I had to prepare for an *even more cruel* world.

Some of my classmates were naked under their thin blue and red gowns, and after we'd sat for half an hour or so on our plastic folding chairs under an overcast sky, a pelting rain began to fall. The wet tee shirt effect this produced did nothing for the solemnity of the occasion. Our principal tried to compare our class to a storm as thunder rolled in the background. Maybe six people clapped when I walked up on the stage—more support than I'd expected, to be honest. To the best of my recollection, I didn't smile or thank whichever administrator handed over my diploma.

CHAPTER 18

AFTERLIFE

In the fall of 2000, several months after graduation and still just 17 years old, I moved to Montreal and started my freshman year at Concordia University. Needless to say, I didn't go there with Sarah—so much for the plans we'd made at age 12, wearing our matching *Blossom*-esque floppy hats. Instead, Tonya and I had enrolled there together. I got accepted into the school's film program and Tonya got accepted into the English department. Still lacking confidence in my ability to make friends on my own, at first I clung to her as my security blanket. It soon became apparent that we didn't need each other to thrive and mature.

That realization began to dawn the day I moved into my dorm room. Carrying an unwieldy stack of two cardboard boxes, I bumped into a boy in the hall. He seemed to be about my age. Instinctively, I started to look away, but he did not. His eyes smiled, and so did his lips. Shocked, I smiled back and kept walking. As I set the boxes down next to my unmade bed, I shook out my tired arms. On my left arm, I had my spiked bracelet and dozens of black sparkly bangles. My fingertips sported black nail polish. My hair was dyed blond with four substantial black chunks. My eyes were still caked in black makeup. I was too stubborn to change my style, which I equated with my essence, but I assumed it meant the sacrifice of a normal young adulthood with a circle of friends. The boy's friendly reaction felt inexplicable.

Before I could head back to my parents' van for another load of belongings, I ran into a friendly, sporty blonde girl with her hair in a ponytail. She smiled and greeted me, not seeming to care how I was dressed.

Nobody did.

Less than a week later I walked past our communal kitchen, thick with smells of toast and ramen, and heard a girl saying, "Gina, yeah, she seems really cool!" It took me a while, but I finally understood that these people weren't just going to tolerate me. They actually liked me. I could relax. There was nothing I had to do to grab their attention, no quirk of my being that had to be sacrificed in order to fit in.

It turned out that starting college was a lot like the experience I'd had at Camp Exploration when I was 14. Communicating with peers ceased to present a challenge. The barrier between my internal voice and the one in my throat rapidly dissolved. It would take me a while to fully open up, but I already seemed to have the basic tools for making friends. I even acquired my first real boyfriend, who loved me and bought me jewelry after a few weeks of dating. He attended an institution in New Hampshire alongside some of my former Spaulding classmates, but even when one of them told him I was the "bomb threat" girl, it didn't affect his feelings for me.

In fact, freshman year turned out to present the opposite problem from the one I'd had in high school, as I partied too hard. At Spaulding, I'd experienced a kind of social death; now I wanted to live for real. Back then I was never invited to any significant parties, and as I've mentioned, Tonya and I lacked access to drugs—unless you count the time we purchased "weed" from a guy downtown, only to end up smoking oregano. At college, where drugs were easy to come by, I found them a useful accessory in social situations. I felt more open to others when I was on ecstasy. On shrooms, my peers and I bonded as we fell into laughing fits, clutching our stomachs at the hilarity of everything and nothing in the world.

If it had been up to me, Tonya and I would have stayed close. Instead, our tie went the way of many adolescent friendships, fading with time although we did stay connected for ten years or so after high school graduation. She moved far away, but we still kept in touch on a regular basis until around 2010. I was using drugs very heavily at the time, and assumed that was the reason she'd vanished, but she later told me she'd felt permanently scarred by our experiences at Spaulding. In response, she wanted to bury all memories of high school, especially the ones that maintaining our connection would threaten to resurrect. I still mourn our friendship and remember it as a highlight of my early life.

As for Sarah, I stopped thinking poorly of her a long time ago. Today, I can even enjoy remembering the good times we had. I simply think she was a terrible match for me, creating a volatile blend that was primed to explode in the post-Columbine atmosphere. Although we've never spoken in the years since, she lives on for me in the sense that I've found myself attracted to friends and romantic partners with whom I've shared a similar dynamic. I'm often too naive in believing that everyone has my best interests at heart. I like to help people, I believe in listening, I want to be a good friend and honestly I can be pretty fucking naive. So, every so often, I fall into the trap of letting myself be bossed around or even bullied. In recent years, I've learned to spot the pattern and change course before the damage mounts.

After I left for college, my parents moved away from Barre. Knowing what Spaulding was like, they didn't want my brother Matt to go there, especially not in the role of younger sibling to an infamous older sister. He already fit the description of a weirdo, and would have been a sitting duck if he'd enrolled in that school. They moved to Essex Junction, Vermont, an upper-middle-class community not far from Burlington. Matt had a good experience there, despite coming out as gay midway through high school. Not everyone was accepting, but most people were, a response I can't picture occurring in the Barre of those years. Nobody came out when I was at Spaulding. I imagine and hope that things are different there now.

My mother's cancer came back and she died in my junior year of college. In the time we had together before her passing, we were able to continue the gradual evolution that had started with the crisis around The Incident, becoming more like friends instead of combative mother and daughter. We talked every day while I was away at Concordia. When she got sick again, she insisted my education needed to come first and wouldn't let me leave school. Only in retrospect have I fully appreciated what a difference her support has made in my life, both on a practical level and in terms of the way she continued to root for me in the worst of times.

For a period in my twenties, I was still preoccupied with impressing some of the people who'd known me at Spaulding. Shortly after attending my ten-year high school reunion, I wound up having a breakdown that landed me in rehab and then in a psych ward, an outcome I'm sure was partially intertwined with unresolved feelings—both guilt and resentment—from my time as a teenage outcast. But those days are now well behind me. I've actually built some real friendships with certain members of the old Barre crowd, undeterred by the animosity we felt in our teen years. Now that I'm without living parents or even much in the way of other family, I find it grounding to keep in touch with these parts of my past.

While I can't say that I had an easy life after high school, one thing that did come easily to me was connecting with others. I learned that my basic nature was sociable. Sarah had convinced me, other classmates had convinced me, and even some teachers had pitched in to help convince me that I lacked any relevant social skills. Most importantly, *I* had fully cooperated in persuading myself that I wasn't a likable person. But the minute I hit college, even the leftover chip on my shoulder couldn't really get in the way of an energetic social life.

Other aspects of my personality began to shine post-high school, and all the shiny parts were the very ones that had made me weird in Barre. I never lost my zest for expressing myself through clothing, and for a time I even worked in the fashion industry. For several years, after moving back to Vermont in my thirties, I served as the director of the state's largest fashion show. Before that, I'd worked in television production, a field I was inspired to break into via my experience at Spaulding's vocational center. Best of all, I was working in mass media, a passion I'd discovered way back in my junior year.

For a long time after high school, Evan stayed in my dreams. Those dreams were always benign, never sexual in nature, and the dreamer teen in me believed it had to mean something. In my mid-twenties, after years of trying not to think about him, I came to the realization that he was linked deeply with my passion for writing, another element of my past that I'd struggled to suppress. I hadn't even kept a journal for years. At this point, I purchased a leather-bound diary and began my first entry with the words, "Dear Chinga." With that, the floodgates opened, and though the process hasn't been simple, I've been writing ever since.

Incredibly, Evan himself re-entered my life a few years later and we began texting every day. We became fast friends, later even moving across the country together and living as roommates. On our cross-country trip we entertained ourselves blasting our old Korn CDs as we drove past mid-western corn fields, even sharing a laugh at the sheer awfulness of the "All in the Family" track the way Tonya and I used to do.

Once, at a literary reading where he was present, and at his suggestion, I read the Elks Club scene in which "Elka" kills "Chinga." I found the murder part less cringe to read in that setting than the juvenile professions of love. He became one of my most devoted friends, and then my best friend and confidante.

And now, he is my husband. I guess I wasn't so delusional after all. He was everything I had imagined he was as a child - deep, intensely smart, caring, and creative —but the reality far exceeded the fantasy. Sometimes I'm haunted by the thought that the ordeal of The Incident likely kept us apart for so many years.

AFTERWORD

On Valentine's Day in 2018, I sat in bed with my spaniel Amelia, a Blenheim Cavalier King Charles, draped over my lap. It felt cozy to have her heating up my legs on a wintry Vermont morning. For the past year I'd been writing true crime content for the online division of the Oxygen television network. This was a dream job for me, since it paid well, allowed me to work remotely (in sweat pants if I so chose!) and, best of all, let me write about homicide.

"There's another shooting," I uttered as I looked through my news feed. Part of my job was monitoring crime reports and writing daily posts about the newsworthy ones.

"*Another* one?" Evan sent over text.

I figured this would be another "small-scale" shooting like the ones in Kentucky and Texas that I'd recently posted about under the heading "2 High School Shootings in Less Than 24 Hours Leave 7 Students Shot, At Least One Dead." Sadly, within hours it was clear that at least 17 people had been killed at Marjory Stoneman Douglas High School in Parkland, Florida. TV coverage of the Winter Olympics in South Korea was interrupted by live footage of reporters quizzing distraught adolescents about the dead bodies they'd just seen. Aerial shots of children fleeing their school, hands frantically waving in the air, gave me goose-bumps and chills. It was Columbine all over again.

In my work as a journalist covering mass killings, it sometimes seems that everything points back to Columbine. That's one reason I've devoted so much time and research effort trying to understand the major issues at play in the public debates over mass shooting violence, for which the horror in Colorado served as a template. One notable aspect is a pattern of politicians seeking to blame school shootings on everything except guns. At a school safety meeting held soon after the Parkland shooting, former president Donald Trump declared that video games, movies, and "the Internet stuff" are the culprits in rampant mass violence. Video games had also been heavily criticized after Columbine, given that the perpetrators had enjoyed playing "Doom," a popular first-person shooter game. Less than a month after Harris and Klebold opened fire with real weapons, Republican Speaker of the House Newt Gingrich declared that "Hollywood and computerized games have undermined the core values of civility."[22] Meanwhile, Bill and Hillary Clinton called for an investigation of the impact of violent content on impressionable teenage minds. Hillary Clinton sponsored a failed bill that sought to criminalize the sale of violent adult games to minors.

It seems almost incredible now, given the heated debates of recent years, that the issue of gun reform received relatively little attention in the Columbine era. It makes me wonder: was all the focus on the supposed dangers of Goth culture basically an avoidance strategy? The fact that the shooters had such easy access to lethal weapons seemed to get lost in the fog of commentary about trench coats and "evil" music and video games and bullying. Defying the odds, a group called Colorado Ceasefire did achieve a small victory by closing a loophole that the Columbine shooters had taken advantage of. It had exempted people purchasing weapons at gun shows from undergoing a background check. A bill to impose more stringent background checks passed in the U.S. Senate, but was defeated in the House.

One of my favorite satirical articles of all time is an *Onion* story entitled "'No Way to Prevent This,' Says Only Nation Where This Regularly Happens." They re-publish it every time there's a mass shooting. I love it because it so succinctly makes what to me is an obvious point: how can this entrenched, all-American refusal to engage in serious gun reform efforts be understood as anything other than a maddening symptom of irresponsibility? If we can recognize the potential of the automobile to function as a deadly weapon, requiring driver education and a test to obtain a license, why can't we do the same for guns? Right now, just about anyone can easily get a state-of-the-art firearm unless they've been convicted of a felony.

Without ready access to guns, it would be impossible for one or two people, acting without accomplices, to quickly slaughter fellow humans en masse. Not that gun control alone can solve the problem; that would likely involve a long, bumpy path. While there have been some advances in gun control law, it always appears to be at a snail's pace and besides even if it were at a rabbit's, I fear it's only a part of the puzzle behind the phenomenon. We Americans are a freakishly violent lot when compared with other wealthy nations. And our mass shootings are growing deadlier. Among other things, this has meant a steady procession of new candidates for the morbid title of "worst shooting in modern American history." Typically it's for people hyper-focused on the sick (and ultra-American) need for infamy, and for going out with a bang. Americans are definitely a strange bunch. There's something deeply embedded in our culture—something that requires honest exploration from a variety of angles, including personal perspectives like the one in this book—that holds out the option of a spectacular mass shooting as a plausible method of making a point.

There has been little priority put on studying the roots of mass murder or even gun violence at all in America in general I've learned. It is an issue that has been neglected for decades.[23] And, to my knowledge, there has been virtually no research into the kind of school shooting adjacent threat world that I was once in; whether or not there is any link between people in my position to real acts of mass violence remains a mystery.

In the wake of the Parkland shooting, I approached various editors with the pitch that much of the live coverage of this fresh tragedy was dangerously reminiscent of the style of television journalism so prevalent in the 1990s. Part of my argument was that Columbine has remained a public fixation for so long because the media's saturation coverage has led to the creation of "an almost sympathetic portrayal of the shooters. To mimic that kind of coverage, to any degree, could possibly result in copycats. School shootings are like fights in schools. One only fuels more. There is a morbid excitement and electricity that surrounds them, a kind of collective blood-thirst."

My concern—based, of course, on my own experience —turned out to be on point. In the wake of the Parkland atrocity, copycat threats have sprouted like weeds. A report published in March, 2018 found that 600 schools across the country had already been targeted.[24] It makes no sense whatsoever to assume that such a phenomenon reflects the fact that hundreds of demon kids have suddenly shed their human skin and embarked on a campaign of mass murder. Surely many of them are misguided, impulsive teens like I was in the wake of Columbine.

My pitch led to a *Daily Dot* op laying out my concerns about the ways in which school shooters are often portrayed. Among other things, I pointed out that white males perpetrators, even mass killers, are often shown in a more sympathetic light than Black shooting victims. It wasn't the first time I'd written about the topic. My goal with these pieces usually included an effort to remind readers of the role played by the infamy conferred by saturation coverage—a poisoned fame not only sought by those actually plotting violent crimes but by a range of alienated or misguided young people caught up in the frenzy.

In 2013, following the terrible events at Sandy Hook Elementary School in Newtown, Connecticut, I'd written a piece for VICE News entitled "I Was a Suspected School Shooter." For the first time, I both publicly acknowledged what I'd done wrong and expressed my pain in an articulate manner. The story went viral and resulted in my receiving dozens of positive messages from people who'd attended Spaulding with me. This was a turning point, since up until it was published some people in Vermont still pigeonholed me as the "bomb threat" girl —even those who didn't know or care very much about the details of what had happened.   In this way, I was able to dispel the thick fog of rumors that still surrounded that part of my past.

I also got an amazing response from people around the world who told me that my story resonated with them. Like me, many had been accused of wanting to shoot up their schools. Some had made death threats. Some had sympathized with killers. But none of them had killed anyone, and they'd eventually matured and come to new understandings.

It made me wonder about the people who'd been sentenced to prison for exactly the type of impulsive gesture that could have landed Tonya and me in far worse trouble if we hadn't lucked out. I wrote to one of them after his mother read my story and reached out to me with a request that I share with him how I'd managed to forgive the people I went to high school with. I told him about my realization that "many who wronged me were mostly broken people to begin with. For example I had numerous female friends that were very close to me that were also very abusive to me. I think sometimes love and hate [go] hand in hand and although I think on some level they loved me very much, they were not raised with love therefore did not know how to show love. All they knew was possession and resentment." I added that I'd had a much harder time forgiving the adults—teachers, administrators, and therapists—who had failed me in major ways. I acknowledged the hurdles the young man was facing. "You have been dealt a terrible injustice. You do not want to become the person that these people want you to be. I did that, and it was a tragedy for me... Anger is a normal reaction. It would be unhealthy, almost, if you didn't have any." As part of my own evolution, I'd come to recognize the ultimately self-destructive consequences of clinging to rage and resentment, no matter the justification. "I don't want to be unhappy anymore," I concluded.

In so many ways, writing has served me as a tremendous tool, not only as an aid to personal healing and growth but a way to engage with public perceptions and thereby, I hope, have a positive impact on a massive social problem that has only proliferated in the years since the Columbine shootings. I feel extremely fortunate that I've had the personal and social resources, not to mention the sheer luck, to be able to maneuver and change my life path. It's still a work in progress. Even when I published the VICE News piece, I knew there were parts of my post-Columbine mindset that I wasn't comfortable going public with.

In 2018, I dug deeper into that darkness in an essay I composed for a graduate writing program I was then enrolled in. For the first time, I admitted to keeping the journal with grainy photos of Eric Harris and Dylan Klebold taped to the inside cover. Narrating in present tense, I dared to re-create my point of view as a lonely, defiant high school senior: *"I do not know it yet but I am aligning myself with mass killers because I believe in a false narrative myself, one that claims that the Columbine killers committed violence because they were victims. I learned later that it's just not true."* The warm response from peers and a faculty member dispelled my lingering anxieties that I'd be ostracized if people in my circle learned who I "really" was. It felt like the granite slab that had been pressing on my heart was lifted away. Nothing I'd done or felt as a teen, no matter how regrettable, ever made me a monster. All along, I was human through and through.

ACKNOWLEDGMENTS

It is nothing short of a miracle that this book has seen the light of day. I am eternally grateful to every single person who helped make this happen.

I am grateful to those who have always championed me in spite of, and sometimes because of, this story.

Thank you to my husband, Ryan Cayia, and my family for loving and supporting me.

Thank you to the loved ones who supported this story before I began drafting this manuscript and to those who rooted for me every step of the way.

Thank you to Miette Gillette and Whisk(e)y Tit for fearlessly giving this book the perfect home and believing in me and my story.

Thank you to authors Chrystin Ondersma, Hillary Leftwich, Jay Halsey, Kim Göransson, Steven Dunn, Freddy La Force, Kim Vodicka, and Bradford Masoni, for never wavering in your support for this book to be published, despite hurdles.

Thank you to the following authors and talented folks, whose keen eyes and smart brains contributed to the editing process: Lily Lalios, Jan Clausen, Caroline Leavitt, Porochista Khakpour, and Roseanne Wells.

I want to thank *VICE* and former *VICE* editor Harry Cheadle for publishing a short-form version of this in 2013 and for naming it one of the best stories of 2013. I am grateful that Longreads put it on a reading list and to other publications for celebrating it, and for receiving the Tarpaulin Sky Book Award for an older version of this manuscript in 2020.

Thank you to anyone who has taken the time to read this, and I hope you have gotten something out of the experience.

ABOUT THE AUTHOR

Gina Tron is the author of several books, including her debut 2014 memoir *You're Fine*, called "vibrant, darkly funny, and courageously candid," by *Interview Magazine*. Her 2020 debut poetry collection, *Star 67*, contains a poem nominated for a Pushcart Prize. She wrote true crime for Oxygen for six years, and wrote and reported pieces for various outlets, including *The Washington Post*, *VICE*, *Politico*, and *The Daily Beast*. In 2015, she collaborated with photographer Jena Cumbo for *We Met On The Internet*, a project called "an anthropological study" by *The New York Times*. Gina's work advocating for rape victim-survivors has helped led to the introduction of several bills and helped lead to the DOJ investigation into the NYPD's Special Victims Department. She received her MFA at Vermont College of Fine Arts and is an adjunct professor at Norwich University in Vermont. You can find more of her work at her website: ginatron.net.

ABOUT THE PUBLISHER

Whisk(e)y Tit is committed to restoring degradation and degeneracy to the literary arts. We work with authors who are unwilling to sacrifice intellectual rigor, unrelenting playfulness, and visual beauty in our literary pursuits, often leading to texts that would otherwise be abandoned in today's largely homogenized literary landscape. In a world governed by idiocy, our commitment to these principles is an act of civil service and civil disobedience alike.

ENDNOTES

1 "The Color of Justice: Racial and Ethnic Disparity in State Prisons." *The Sentencing Project.* 2021.

2 Wrenger, Daniel. "Pearl Jam's 'Jeremy' and the Intractable Cultural Script of School Shooters." *The New Yorker.* 2016.

3 Bjorkqvist, Lagerspetz, & Kaukiainen, 1992; Wang, Iannotti, & Nansel, 2009.

4 Oliker, Ditta M. Ph.D., "Bullying in the Female World." *Psychology Today.* Sept. 2011.

5 Glaberson, William. "Finding Futility in Trying to Lay Blame in Killings." *The New York Times.* Aug. 2000.

6 Tapper, Jake and Avery Miller. "Teacher Warned Authorities About Va. Tech Shooter." ABC News. Apr. 2007.

7 "Who are the Trenchcoat Mafia?" *BBC.* April 1999.

8 Chen, Stephanie. ""Debunking the myths of Columbine, 10 years later." *CNN.* April 2009.

9 Jacobson, Mark. "The Generation Gap in My Living Room." *New York Magazine.* May 1999.

10 Patterson-Neubert, Amy. "Study: Columbine news coverage misled nation down fearful road." *Perdue News.* April 2003.

11 Tron, Gina. "Criminologist And FBI To Journalists: Stop Naming Mass Murderers." *Oxygen.* Dec. 2017.

12 Klebold, Sue. "A Mother's Reckoning: Living in the Aftermath of Tragedy." Random House. 2016.

13 Cullen, Dave. "Columbine Killer Eric Harris Plans the Massacre." *Slate Magazine*, Slate, 16 Apr. 2009

14 Cullen, Dave. *Columbine*. Grand Central Publishing, 2010.

15 Langman, Peter. "Statistics on Bullying and School Shootings." SchoolShooters.info. Nov. 2014

16 King, Stephen. *On Writing: A Memoir of the Craft*. Scribner. 2000.

17 Katz, Jon. Geeks: How Two Lost Boys Rode the Internet Out of Idaho. Crown. 2001.

18 Ingersoll, Geoffrey. "The Antipsychotic Prescribed To Adam Lanza Has A Troubled HIstory All Its Own." *Business Insider.* Dec. 2018.

19 Welch, Ashley. "Study reveals how many U.S. adults are taking psychiatric drugs." CBS News. Dec. 2016.

20 Christensen, Doreen and Brittany Wallman. "Crazed girls flood Parkland school shooter Nikolas Cruz with fan mail." *Sun Sentinel*. March, 2018.

21 Klebold, Sue. A Mother's Reckoning: Living in the Aftermath of Tragedy. Crown. 2016.

22 Disis, Jill. "The long history of blaming video games for mass violence." *CNN*. March 2018.

23 Corujo, Christina and Jessie DiMartino. "Decadeslong gap in gun violence research funding has lasting impact." *ABC News.* Nov. 2021.

24 Hayes, Christal. "After Florida shooting, more than 600 copycat threats have targeted schools." *USA Today*. Mar. 2018.

www.ingramcontent.com/pod-product-compliance
Ingram Content Group UK Ltd.
Pitfield, Milton Keynes, MK11 3LW, UK
UKHW032334131224
452011UK00005B/69

9 781952 600586